Caxton's
History of the World
Volume Sixteen

THE NINETEENTH CHALLENGE CENTURY OF THE

Advisory Editor
Esmond Wright
former Professor of Modern History
at the University of Glasgow

Text by
John Burnett

New Caxton Library Service

Based on original French work
Connaissance de l'Histoire © 1967
Librairie Hachette
Illustrations © 1967 Librairie Hachette
English text © 1969 The Hamlyn
Publishing Group Ltd
SBN 6001 3940 9
First English edition 1969
Phototypeset by Oliver Burridge
Filmsetting Ltd, Crawley, Sussex
Printed in France by Brodard et Taupin,
Paris, for The Hamlyn Publishing Group
Ltd, London, New York, Sydney, Toronto,
The Centre, Feltham, Middlesex, England
Special Edition for
New Caxton Library Service Ltd · London

Contents

Introduction   6

The new Europe   9

The old Europe
Great estates and small farms
Industrial Europe
The revolution in transport
The conquering bourgeoisie
The disinherited
Reformers and utopians
The triumph of science
The romantic age
England after Waterloo
Parliamentary aristocracy
The two Englands
The postwar depression
Scandals at court
Middle-class reform
The Great Reform Bill of 1832
The new poor law
The beginning of the Victorian Age
The other nation
The Chartist challenge
The triumph of free trade
The British Empire
British India
The white empire
Origins of the Commonwealth
Britain's achievement

The springtime of nations   43

The peoples and the Holy Alliance
Germany: the Congresses of Carlsbad
   and Vienna
Revolutions in Cadiz and Naples
Troppau and Laibach: reaction in Italy
The Congress of Verona: repression
   in Spain
The revolution of 1830 and the rise of
   Mazzini
Germany and Poland
The birth of modern Belgium
The crisis of 1848
The revolution in Italy
The revolution in Austria
Failure in Italy: the march of Radetzky
The defeat of the Austrian revolution
The agony of Hungary
Defeat in Germany
The Eastern Question
The awakening of Greece
The savage war

The intervention of the powers: Navarino
The Egypt of Mehemet Ali
The first Syrian War
The second Syrian War
The dispute over the Holy Places
The 'Sick Man of Europe'
The Crimean War: Sebastopol
The Peace of Paris

Russia: the years of conflict   75

Reaction and the Holy Alliance
The Decembrists
Autocracy and orthodoxy
The new Russia
The intelligentsia
The consequences of the Crimean War
Alexander II and the abolition of
   serfdom
Liberal reform
The young revolutionaries
The Polish insurrection
Reaction in Russia
The expansion of the Russian Empire
The economic development of Russia
The standard of living
Urban Russia

France from the Restoration
to Napoleon III   93

The restoration of the Bourbons
The *Chambre Introuvable*
The constitutionalists in power
Villèle and the reaction
Charles X: from Villèle to Polignac
The glorious days of 1830
The victory of the Orléanists
The July Monarchy
The revolt of the silk workers
The republican opposition
The ministry of Guizot
The revolution of 1848
The two flags
The April elections
The National Workshops
The days of June
The return of Louis Bonaparte
The Conservative Republic
The *coup d'état* of December 1851
'The empire is peace'
The aristocratic empire
Parisian life
The Orsini affair
The liberal empire
The parliamentary empire

Further Reading List   126

Acknowledgments   126

Index   127

Introduction By ESMOND WRIGHT

When in 1815 Louis XVIII returned for a second time to the throne of the Bourbons it seemed that an ugly and violent chapter in European history was at last closed. Although the French had again revealed their political instability by the enthusiasm they had shown for Napoleon Bonaparte when he escaped from Elba in March 1815, he was now safely incarcerated on St Helena deep in the South Atlantic and could not escape again; and the very moderation of the peace terms on which the British foreign secretary, Castlereagh, insisted seemed to promise an opportunity for good sense to prevail after the twenty years of conflict. These hopes were reinforced by the conciliatory mood of Louis XVIII. He was declared king 'by the grace of God', and he graciously presented a royal charter to his grateful people. But he was wise enough to include in it the concession of those civil rights and rights to property which had been the permanent result of the Revolution, and which had been won the hard way. The hope was for constitutional government on British lines.

Yet the form was clear: the watchword of the Congress of Vienna was 'legitimacy', even if the case for the restoration of the legitimate rulers and their descendants was that it was in the people's best interests. 'The principle of legitimacy', wrote Talleyrand to Louis XVIII, 'must be held sacred in the interest of the people themselves, because legitimate governments can alone be strong and durable, whereas illegitimate governments, relying upon force only, fall to pieces the moment that support fails them, and then the people are delivered over to a succession of revolutions of which no one can foresee the end.'

And so, for a variety of reasons, the Concert of Europe was born. The French foreign minister, Talleyrand, wanted to restore the pre-revolutionary map of Europe and get the best possible terms for France, Metternich dreaded a new wave of revolution lest it further weaken the diverse and chequered Habsburg Empire. Hardenberg for Prussia shared his fears. Alexander I of Russia, alternating between moods of repression and liberalism, sought a union with his fellow rulers 'as members of a single Christian nation' and opposed whatever might thwart it. And Castlereagh's objective was primarily to re-create a power balance in a Europe torn and destroyed by a generation of war, so that his island empire could absorb her widely scattered conquests to which

there could now be no European challenge. Along with 'legitimacy' went the 'compensations'. And by them Britain did well indeed. She dominated the key strategic points—and the coaling stations for the coming age of steam—on all the oceans. For two generations she was the political and industrial pace-setter for the world.

It is easy now in retrospect to see how false were some of these assumptions and how short-lived the post-1815 stability. Yet the Holy Alliance and the conferences of the post-1815 years saw for the first time a genuine attempt to manufacture by diplomacy a European concert of power. It was for a purpose: the suppression at source of the first signs of unrest. Revolutions were put down by force, at speed and by foreign intervention: in 1819 in Germany, in 1821 in Italy, in 1823 in Spain, in 1830 in Italy, in 1831 in Poland and in many countries in 1848-9. In 1830, in 1848 and in 1870 the barricades were raised in Paris; and throughout the period unrest and violence were endemic in Russia. There was no peace. When Metternich fled in 1848, there was still his replica, Schwartzenberg, to reign in his place. But, except in 1827 in Greek waters and in 1854 in the Crimea, there was no war in Europe either. The diplomats relied on the exhaustion of Europe, on the passiveness of a heavily rural society and on military force. And from their experiences they could hardly have acted otherwise. They ignored however the social and economic forces, the fact that the movement of armies carried with it the movement also of ideas, the growth of population, the development of railways, telegraph and postal services, the appearance in each country of a middle class that was the product of city life, commerce and schools, that would now permanently break the aristocratic pattern and begin to grope towards an Internationale of trade. Metternich was intelligent, shrewd, every inch a realist, utterly devoid of Alexander's mysticism. He recognised, and was right to do so, the fragile character of human society. His ideal was limited, but in its way noble. He laboured hard to maintain the equilibrium of Europe; as he wrote in 1824 Europe 'has acquired for me the quality of one's own country'. He was remarkably successful. He held the fort until 1848. But he ignored the three new creative and disruptive elements that were to make the years between the fall of Napoleon I and the rise of Bismarck so exciting; the industrial revolution, and the forces of nationalism and socialism.

The industrial revolution was of course very uneven in its impact. Europe as a whole was still rural; serfdom was abolished in France in 1789 and in Prussia in 1807. But the effects of the abolition were varied. If small peasant farms became characteristic of western Europe, in the lands east of the Elbe a large, landless, agricultural labouring class was produced. And in Russia in 1815 there were still 16,000,000 serfs on the Crown lands alone. Dr Burnett makes very clear in his text the acute problems posed by serfdom to the Tsars, the difficulty of finding any solution for it, yet the unrest and instability in Russia until this problem was solved.

It was to this overwhelmingly rural world that the industrial revolution came. It came first in Britain and spread to western Europe: it was British capital and companies which applied steam to transportation on land and sea in France as well as Britain, so that a spider-like spread of railway lines appeared on the map of Europe between 1830 and 1870; coal and factory production boomed because of the use of steam engines. Ghent and Brussels, Liège and Lille, Namur and the Ruhr, Manchester and Glasgow, became industrial centres of textiles, metallurgy, coal and steel.

The results were evident in the population boom—there was a five-fold increase in the British population between 1814 and 1914, and London grew from 875,000 to 2,000,000 in the years from 1800 to 1850 and to 5,000,000 by 1900; Cologne and Paris doubled in population in the same period; in 1800 there were 22 towns in Europe with more than 100,000 population; by 1850 there were 47. There was also a series of cholera and typhus epidemics leading to a campaign for a public health service. Interest grew in wider and larger markets (hence the emphasis on the Empire of Britain and on the Union of the German States), state education and scientific invention, and the development of joint stock companies. Napoleon was in nothing quite so far-sighted as in his commercial code, which was adopted throughout most of western Europe; he was far more modern-minded than Metternich or Castlereagh.

Industrially, Britain was half a century ahead of Europe. She produced 10,000,000 tons of coal in 1800, 56,000,000 tons a year by 1850. This process did not occur in France until the years of the Second Empire: coal and iron production trebled between 1850 and 1870. And by 1871, aided by victory, Germany was, by rapid scientific training, outdistancing France. By 1871, though few appreciated this, the British dominance was over. In the sixty years between 1850 and 1910 iron production trebled in Britain, rose six-fold in France, but twenty-six-fold in Germany.

The same forces were at work in agriculture, with improvement in farming techniques, the abandonment of the fallow land system, the use of fertilisers, the specialisation of crops, and the cross-breeding of cattle.

And behind all these developments was money, not least in London, Paris and Amsterdam. Krupp was typical of one aspect of the industrial growth. What in 1826 was a near-bankrupt household business had become by 1870 a vast, private, paternalist empire of steel and bronze and guns, with pension schemes, hotels and stores—and no trade unions. The five Rothschild brothers from the Frankfurt ghetto managed the banking houses of Frankfurt, Vienna, London, Paris and Naples. When the transfer of funds over such distances was dangerous they could act as one and speedily, and with confidence and trust. They invested shrewdly, especially in railways and shipping. They became barons of the Austrian Empire and assisted Disraeli over Suez, but they never overcame either envy of their skill or prejudice against their race. Yet, as their careers showed, and as did Disraeli's, it was possible to climb up the greasy pole, whatever your origins, your accent or your race. It was easier in Britain than in Europe. Or rather it was not easy at all: but it could be done.

Metternich's vision of Europe had a certain nobility—seen at least in the light of the problems of today. But it foundered, as did the fortunes of the Habsburg house he served, not only on indifference to economics but on ignorance of the emotional force of nationalism. So did the cause of aristocracy. For the early nineteenth century was held together in its internationalism by the existence of a class whose manners were stylised, whose language was French and whose loyalties were less to territory and nation than to a sovereign. The chancellor of the German Empire in 1894, Hohenlohe, had a brother who was an official of the emperor Joseph of Austria, another on service in Prussia, and yet another at the Papal Court in Rome. Their loyalties were personal. The coming of the bourgeoisie meant the emergence of nationalism. Honour now became national, and nations began to take offence, to meet challenges that had been seen until then as purely personal. And the nationalism itself passed from the romantic and cultural force that it was to Chateaubriand and Mazzini to a hard, scientific, military force—a product of Darwin. The test of national honour by 1870 was conflict, and the national concept was in the process brutalised, coarsened and devalued. Nationalist symbols and legendry grew, not least in Britain and the United States. But of its emotional power there could be no question. Loyalty was no longer to king or lord, class or creed, but to the republic one and indivisible. It became synonymous with notions of the rights of men and the career open to talent. It would be defended not by a professional class of warriors but by all its citizens. And it was for export. Belgium won its independence in 1830; Italy as a nation became more than a 'geographical expression'; each component part of the Austrian Empire struggled for self-determination; poets and historians kept alive the sparks of independence in Prague and Budapest, Belgrade and Athens. Greece won its independence and the map of the Balkans became a jigsaw of ever-changing boundaries. For every little language felt that it had to have a country all its own. Nationalism was a force that later both Bismarck and Hitler could exploit. And beyond nationalism was imperialism and the notion of the raj. By 1870, with the Suez Canal cut and a quick road open to India, an imperial age was about to be born.

But the major force that emerged in these years was Socialism itself. Before long class would compete with nation for loyalty and allegiance, and some of the most difficult tensions and problems of our own time would come to birth. In the pages that follow Dr Burnett describes them clearly and vividly.

BRITAIN IN THE EARLY NINETEENTH CENTURY

	Great Britain	British colonies	Scientific progress
1815	Corn law (1815) Widespread distress and economic depression Peterloo Massacre (1819) Death of George III; accession of George IV (1820) Cato Street Conspiracy (1820)	Revolt against British rule in Ceylon —suppressed (1817) Singapore founded (1819)	First steamship crosses the Atlantic (1819)
1820			
1825	Canning foreign minister (1822)	Gold Coast becomes a crown colony (1821) Britain acquires Malacca (1824)	Stephenson builds first iron railway bridge (1823) Stockton-Darlington railway opens (1825)
1830	Duke of Wellington prime minister (1828) Sliding scale of duties on imported corn (1828) Catholic Emancipation Act (1829) Death of George IV; accession of William IV (1830)		Niepce makes photograph on a metal plate (1827) G. S. Ohm defines electrical current, potential and resistance
1835	Whig government under Earl Grey (1830) Reform Act (1832) Abolition of slavery in British colonies (1833) Robert Owen's Grand National Consolidated Trades Union (183–4) Tolpuddle Martyrs (1834)	Revolt in Jamaica (1831) Falkland Islands become a crown colony (1833) St Helena a crown colony (1834)	Construction of first U.S. railway (1832) Faraday's laws on electrolysis (1834) Samuel Colt patents his revolver (1835)
1840	Death of William IV; accession of Queen Victoria (1837) Chartist petition rejected by Parliament (1839)	Great Trek in South Africa; Orange Free State republic founded (1836) Rebellion in Canada (1837) Boers defeat Zulus at Blood River (1838) Act of Union in Canada (1840)	Samuel Morse develops telegraph (1837) Daguerre discovers daguerrotype process (1838)
1845	Robert Peel prime minister (1841) Chartist riots in Lancashire: second Chartist petition to Parliament rejected (1842) Bank Charter Act (1844)	New Zealand becomes a separate colony; Maori insurrection (1841) South Australia a crown colony (1841) Natal becomes a British colony (1843)	First use of general anaesthetic in an operation (1842) First screw-steamer crosses the Atlantic (1843)
1850	Repeal of the Corn Laws (1846) Failure of Chartist Movement (1848) Famine in Ireland	Responsible government in Canada (1846) Establishment of Orange River Sovereignty (1848) Annexation of Punjab (1849)	Sewing-machine invented (1846) Aneroid barometer designed (1847) Steam threshing machine invented (1850)

The new Europe

The aftermath of the Napoleonic Wars: England after Waterloo; the industrial revolution; the Victorian Age and the expansion of the British Empire.

A man born in 1815 might reasonably have expected to live until 1870. Had he done so, he would have witnessed more changes— political, economic, industrial and social— than in any comparable period in history. While the Europe of 1870 was recognisably modern, that of 1815 was still in many respects medieval. After more than twenty years of revolution, war and destruction the old order was restored by the victors of Waterloo, and the deep cracks which had seemed to be breaking up the structure of European society in 1789 were temporarily pasted over. Except in France, the lot of the peasant had scarcely changed, and the land which still formed the basis of the European economy continued to be tilled in the same laborious way that it had for centuries past. But the apparent continuity with the past was only superficial, and from about 1830 onwards scientific progress and social change accelerated spectacularly. Develop-

ments in industry, commerce and trade brought vast new wealth to western Europe, but at the same time created a rootless working class and an intellectual protest that was ultimately to shatter the old order so carefully reconstructed in 1815. The lasting revolution was to be an economic, not a political one, its home England, not France.

The old Europe

At the beginning of the nineteenth century Europe remained essentially agricultural, and as in all agricultural societies, life was directly affected by the state of the harvest. The absence of any permanent crop surpluses seriously hampered economic development: seasonal and annual crises, traceable to weather conditions, inadequate commercial organisation and transport systems, were followed at the end of the wars by a long period of falling prices which

afforded no encouragement to change of any kind. With a few exceptions, agricultural techniques remained backward and unchanging. Great aristocratic landowners, uninterested in the processes of farming, were content to draw rents from their tenants and to value their estates in terms of the social status and political power that they conferred. Small farmers, though they might have the will to experiment and make changes, could rarely command the capital necessary to do so.

Throughout most of Europe, cultivation was still by the primitive methods of the Middle Ages. For lack of fertilisers land had to be kept fallow one year in every three, and

The new steamboat Église *in front of the old royal palace of the Tuileries in 1815. (Bibliothèque Nationale, Paris.)*

much still lay in uncultivated waste: seed was sown 'broadcast' by hand, reaping was by scythe and threshing by flail. Crop yields were low, and undernourished animals, left to fend for themselves on rough pastures and commons, prevented any progress in scientific stock-breeding. The absence of developed communications and means of storing food compelled each country—and, often, each district—to be as self-supporting as possible, and it was only in a few luxury foods such as spices, sugar, coffee and tea that there was any important foreign trade.

Yet the first half of the nineteenth century was to see impressive agricultural progress, spurred on by growing populations and increasing demands for food. Change had begun in England in the previous century, where 'improving' landlords had enclosed scattered holdings into compact farms, had introduced new rotational systems based on the use of root-crops, and had greatly increased the size and weight of animals by selective breeding. Such practices became more widespread during the Napoleonic Wars, and enabled England not only to survive the French blockade but to feed a population that grew threefold, from 6,000,000 to 18,000,000, during the century 1750–1850.

By the 1840s steam-ploughs and steam-threshers were coming to replace the labour of man, manure and artificial fertilisers (discovered by the German chemist Liebig) were enriching the soil and increasing yields, while the drainage of heavy clay lands, made possible by the mass-production of nonporous pipes, was bringing ever more land under the plough. Altogether these changes meant a fundamental break with the past and a new concept of landownership for profit rather than pleasure.

Great estates and small farms

Outside England there were two main types of agriculture in Europe. In France, the Low Countries, Switzerland and Northern Italy the suppression of feudal servitude had emancipated the peasants, but had resulted in a pattern of small and medium-sized farms which were economically unable to take advantage of the new and costly agricultural techniques.

Elsewhere in Europe, vast manorial estates remained typical. In Southern Italy the landowning aristocracy practised absenteeism, leaving the management of their estates to stewards who let it out to tenant-farmers often at exorbitant rents. Spanish lords also leased out their lands, but were restricted by the *Mesta*, the powerful association of sheep-farmers who monopolised vast areas of pasturage and were opposed to the development of arable farming.

In Prussia and eastern Europe the Napoleonic reforms were also abandoned soon after Waterloo, and peasants who had acquired land were now often compelled to restore part of it. On some Prussian estates,

however, there was evidence of agricultural improvement on the English model, in contrast to the medieval conditions that still prevailed in Russia. Here, the land was owned entirely by the Crown and nobility: landowners kept back part for their own use, and let the rest to serfs in small plots in return for payments and obligations of many kinds. Although Russia was the largest exporter of wheat in Europe, it was at the expense of a population that lived permanently close to starvation level. This contrast between eastern and western Europe, based on the different systems of land-ownership, resulted in glaring economic divisions which were to survive until recent times.

Industrial Europe

The new Europe—the Europe of machines and factories, railways and steam-engines—was hardly evident in 1815. Only in England, where industrialisation had been growing at an increasing pace since the middle of the eighteenth century, were the changes clearly visible. Here, a small population had responded to a great overseas demand by mechanisation, first of the spinning and weaving of textiles, next of the manufacture of iron and steel, and then of the actual means of power. Whether the British people had any peculiar inventive skill over other nations is doubtful: it is more likely that the industrial revolution began there because of a particular combination of circumstances —economic, social and political—that could not be found elsewhere at the time. But the fact was that the discoveries of Hargreaves (the spinning jenny) and Arkwright (an early spinning machine driven by water power), of Watt (the steam-engine), Cort (a process for purifying iron) and a score of others, were not only turning England into the wealthiest and most powerful nation in the world, but were ultimately to start a revolution throughout Europe, the consequences of which are still not fully worked out.

Britain, admittedly, had certain natural elements which favoured her early industrialisation—coal and iron in great quantity

German industry grew rapidly during the first half of the nineteenth century.
Above: a factory in the Ruhr in 1815.
(Zeughaus, East Berlin.)
Above left: an early iron foundry.
(Nationalgalerie, East Berlin.)
The transport revolution. In 1848 Britain had nearly 5,000 miles of railway compared with 2,500 miles in Prussia.
Left: the railway near Nuremberg.
(Bibliothèque Nationale, Paris.)

and easily accessible, an old-established cloth industry which supplied a basis of organisational knowledge and experience, a vast colonial market for her goods, a developed banking system and a political structure that encouraged freedom and individual initiative. Before 1830, industrialisation in France made only slow headway, delayed by poor communications and banking institutions, and by the continuation of protectionist policies that only hampered progress. Here, the pace of change quickened noticeably after the accession of Louis Philippe: the iron industry developed rapidly under iron masters like Schneider at Creusot and Wendel in Lorraine, the number of steam-engines in use doubled within six years, while the number of power-looms in Alsace and Normandy increased seven-fold between 1830 and 1848.

In Germany, the 'take-off' into industrialisation was even slower. In 1830 the Ruhr was still a predominantly agricultural region, and Krupp, the great armament

manufacturer of the future, employed only nine workers: such industrial centres as existed were situated close to the ironfields of Saxony, the Saar, Upper Silesia and Bohemia. Only towards 1840 did the more intensive exploitation of coal fields and steam-power indicate the real beginnings of technological advance. In Belgium, too, money from the aristocracy was by now beginning to stimulate the heavy industries in the valleys of the Meuse and Sambre.

Elsewhere in Europe there was, as yet, little sign of industrial progress. Some Italian cities were famous, as they had been for centuries past, for high quality workmanship in silk, leather and precious metals, but these were small-scale craft industries carried on in much the same way as they had been since medieval times. Here, as in Germany and other European states, the development of trade was seriously hampered by political divisions and the survival of local monopolies controlled by guilds and city corporations.

In spite of such impediments, it is likely that total European industrial output doubled between 1815 and 1848. Yet the progress of early capitalism was uneven, marked by booms and slumps which implied an inadequate adaptation to the market forces of supply and demand. Most countries attempted to protect their economies by complicated systems of tariffs and import restrictions which only served to keep down the total level of international trade. Such ideas were increasingly coming under attack from economists like Ricardo, Say and Mill who, deriving their theories from Adam Smith's *The Wealth of Nations* (1776), argued that wealth would be greatly increased if each country concentrated on producing what it was best fitted for by nature (whether food or manufactures) and then exchanged freely with all other nations. In the absence of artificial controls, production would always adjust itself to demand through the agency of the price mechanism.

Free trade found its first expression in

Transport before the railway age. Among the first bicycles was the draisine *(below left) originated in 1816 by Baron von Sauerbronn, chief forester of the duchy of Baden, to use on his inspection tours. It was gradually improved until in 1865 Pierre Lallemant introduced the* velocipede *or 'penny farthing' (far left) running on iron-tyred wooden rims, the front wheel being larger than the rear. (Bibliothèque Nationale, Paris.)*
Left: urban transport—traffic in front of a theatre at Dahlem, near Berlin. (Stamp Office, West Berlin.)
Below: the horse remained the principal means of communication, both for work and leisure. (Bibliothèque Nationale, Paris.)

Railways gave rise to fears for the safety of passengers. It was said that the transport of soldiers by train would make them effeminate, and that the tunnel at Saint-Cloud would cause 'inflammation of the lungs, pleurisy and catarrh'. Early carriages were designed as closely as possible to resemble stagecoaches, partly to reassure passengers.

Below: an early French railway.
Below centre: the railway at Versailles.
Water transport was also changing—steamboats in fact preceded the steam locomotive.
Right: before the invention of the propeller paddlewheels were used.
Bottom: the new Regent's Canal, London. It was opened in 1820.
(Bibliothèque Nationale, Paris.)

England, where a gradual process of tariff or Customs duty reduction was begun in the 1820s by Huskisson and continued by Peel in the 1840s. Its most spectacular success came in 1846 with the repeal of the Corn Laws, and the removal of the protection from wheat imports which farmers had long enjoyed: England would hereafter buy her food in the cheapest markets of the world, and live by her manufactures.

The revolution in transport

Industrialisation required a fast and efficient system of communications for the movement of men, materials and goods. During the latter half of the eighteenth century, England had already made important developments in mobility by the construction of canals for the movement of heavy goods and the improvement of road surfaces for the transport of passengers. On the turnpike roads of Brindley, Telford and Macadam stagecoaches could carry twenty passengers at speeds of up to fifteen miles an hour.

The decisive change came with the steam locomotive, first successfully developed by George Stephenson in 1814. Originally, it was seen merely as a means of speeding up the transport of coal from mines, and the first railways, such as the Stockton to Darlington in England and the Saint-Etienne to Andrezième in France, were intended solely for industrial purposes.

But by 1830 Stephenson had produced a locomotive which could travel at thirty miles an hour, and the use of steel rails, automatic brakes and improved coaches made people aware of the railway's great potential for passenger transport. A 'railway mania' in England resulted in the formation of hundreds of private companies, some of them economically unsound but many paying handsome dividends to shareholders. By 1850 almost all the principal towns had been linked by some 6,000 miles of rail, the average cost of which had been £56,000 per mile.

In other countries, development was retarded by distrust and the opposition of vested interests. Hostility came from landowners, coaching establishments and innkeepers—above all, sufficient capital was not forthcoming from investors who preferred to put their money into land or safe government securities. Despite campaigns led by the banker Péreire and the economist Chevalier, the French network really only began after 1837, the first line, Paris to Saint-Germain, being sponsored by Baron Rothschild. Although it was an immediate success, there were still only 2,000 miles of French railways in 1848.

Railway construction followed in Belgium, Germany, Italy and in many countries throughout the world, often directed by British engineers and carried out by British workmen. In Germany the railway had a particular importance in the development of the *Zollverein*—the customs union by which

The development of capitalism tended to sharpen the divisions in society between plenty and want. On one hand the great wealth of the nobility was now joined by that of the new middle classes.
Above right: the great castle of Charlottenburg, near Berlin. The castle was built in 1696 for Sophie Charlotte, wife of the elector Frederick. A fine collection of antiques and paintings is on view there today. (Stamp Office, West Berlin.)
Far right: a grand reception given for the centenary of the foundation of The Order of Maria Theresa. (Schönbrunn, Vienna.)
On the other hand, industrialisation created a miserable working class, divorced from the ownership of property and the means of production, whose plight aroused the sympathy of philosophers such as the Count of Saint-Simon (above). An early socialist, he advocated the creation of an industrial society in which all classes would share ownership and control. (Bibliothèque Nationale, Paris.)

Prussia was gradually forging a nation out of a collection of independent states: in 1850 Germany had some 3,500 miles of track and a great continental line from Aachen to Hanover and Berlin.

The economic and social effects of railways were revolutionary. Journeys were shortened from days to hours; the cost of moving goods was halved and the market for them vastly expanded; perishable foods in particular received a new mobility, and could now be transported into the rapidly growing urban centres in good condition. Railways broke down the isolation of centuries, and compelled people whose horizons had previously been bounded by the village to think in terms of the nation: although they were a socially binding force it is probably true to say that they were a nationally divisive one.

But it is not in dispute that steam locomotion—whether by land or by the new steamships that were now crossing the Atlantic in seventeen days instead of forty—was one of the most powerful forces shaping modern civilisation. Where the rail was laid, telegraph systems were constructed alongside, news and letters could be carried cheaply and swiftly, and national daily papers became possible. The new mobility that was thus given to the movement of ideas was at least as important as that conferred on people and goods.

The conquering bourgeoisie

Rich and poor there had always been, but industrialisation tended to exaggerate the differences between plenty and want, to make the extremes more conspicuous, more exposed to public envy and concern. In countries which had not yet felt the impact of industrial change, the traditional two-tier system of aristocratic landowners and landless peasants persisted—in Southern Italy and in parts of Prussia and Russia, where social and political influence was still exclusively in the hands of a tiny territorial aristocracy.

However, in the industrially developing parts of Europe a third, middle class was rapidly rising to power and wealth, a class distinguished by their manipulation of capital rather than by ownership of land. These were the bankers and merchants of the new professions that complex financial undertakings and business relationships called into existence. At the extremities they merged imperceptibly into the classes above and below them; there was no single middle class, rather an infinite series of gradations. What characterised them, and distinguished them sharply from their social inferiors, was the ownership of capital or means of production on which they could employ others to work, or the possession of special professional skills usually derived from some form of advanced education.

At the summit of the middle classes, barely distinguishable in wealth from the landed aristocracy, was the financial elite—a relatively few great families whose business lay in the use (to some the abuse) of money. These were the banking and financial houses, which dealt in money lending on a grand scale, government credit, the discounting of bills of exchange and speculation in mining and the precious metals.

A general shortage of currency (still based on gold and silver) at a time of expanding trade, as well as the inadequate development of banking facilities, favoured such activities and their concentration into a few hands. Banking houses like the Barings in England, the Hopes in Amsterdam and the Rothschilds with a family network extending through five European capitals, rivalled the wealth and influence of dukes and princes. The Jewish origins of some prevented their complete social acceptance, yet others were ennobled, became leading patrons of the arts and were famous for their lavish entertaining and hospitality.

Below the merchant princes were the upper middle-classes—the owners of textile factories and iron-works, the leading members of the professions and public administration, the army officers and diplomatic officials. Socially they were of mixed origins. Government service and army were still recruited mainly from the younger sons of nobility who, because of the rule of primogeniture, would not succeed to their fathers' estates: patronage assured them of remunerative sinecures, the actual work of which was done by poorly paid clerks. But in the ranks of the industrialists were found members of the *nouveaux riches*, men of often humble origins who had carved their way to fortune by hard work, thrift and an unusual degree of intelligence or good fortune.

These various elements had in common the enjoyment of a degree of affluence which provided them with fine houses in the fashionable quarters and suburbs of the towns, armies of domestic servants who relieved their wives of all the household duties, and enabled them to educate and provide for their children. Above all, they shared a thirst for political power, a dislike of the aristocracy and a distrust of the working classes, a belief in free trade and free enterprise as the keys to economic success both for themselves and for the nation as a whole.

In the more advanced countries of western Europe they were already making a bid for power, and beginning to break the domination of the landed gentry. In England the middle classes were enfranchised by the Reform Act of 1832, and through the newly formed Conservative Party of Robert Peel won a remarkable success with the abolition of the Corn Laws in 1846: similarly the accession in 1830 of Louis Philippe, 'the bourgeois king', was the beginning of a period of increased power and influence for the French middle classes.

There were no over-night revolutions. Aristocratic power remained deeply entrenched, and even in England it was not until 1880 that middle-class members constituted a majority in the House of Commons: the important thing was that a shift in economic power was gradually bringing about a major political change and was causing a mounting attack on the aristocracy, its power and privileges.

The disinherited

In his famous work *Das Kapital*, first published in 1867, Karl Marx stated his belief that industrialisation inevitably tended to divide society into two opposing groups of employers and employees, those who possessed capital and those who did not, and that the issue between them could be resolved only by revolution. To many observers in the first half of the nineteenth century his gloomy prediction seemed fully justified. Even in the wealthy western countries of Europe agricultural labourers, who still constituted the majority of the population in 1815, lived in destitution and semi-starvation, existing on a diet of bread, cheese and vegetables, with meat a rare luxury. Meagre wages were supplemented by the earnings of wives and children as soon as they were old enough to work at field-labour or domestic occupations like spinning and weaving.

In England the land enclosure movement had created a class of landless labourers entirely dependent on the wages paid by farmers. Elsewhere in Europe, small peasant farms had remained, but under such difficult conditions that the tenants had a constant struggle to escape from the extortions of landlords and money-lenders. Riots and risings were common occurrences in Russia, southern Germany and Ireland, and were not unknown even in the 'peaceful' English countryside.

All over Europe there was a steady migration into the towns. Whether men felt dispossessed from the land or attracted by the greater opportunities of town life is difficult to say, and it is still impossible to draw up an accurate balance-sheet of the gains and losses which such a transition involved. In factories and mines wages twice and three times as high as those of the agricultural labourer could be earned. On the other hand, workers had to submit to the impersonal discipline of the mill, to accept a working day of fourteen or fifteen hours, often in over-heated and insanitary conditions, and to live in crowded slums where they were shut out from the familiar peace and beauty of nature.

The employment of children from the age of five or six upwards in such conditions was a new and special evil which ultimately excited public concern and control, but the inhuman conditions under which thousands of men and women had to work—the tyranny and brutality of petty masters and overseers, the disease and early death that factory life often brought about, the drunkenness, immorality and prostitution that were all too common in the industrial town—seemed to pass almost unnoticed.

In England, Belgium and France the spontaneous reaction of workers to such conditions was often to break the machines that appeared to be depriving them of their livelihood. These 'Luddite' risings, like the sporadic strikes which were a common feature of early industrial society, were suppressed with great severity—none more so than that of the Lyons silk-weavers, which resulted in a thousand deaths. In the absence of effective trade unions such actions were doomed to failure. The only form of workers' associations which had any success in the period were the peaceful friendly societies formed by skilled craftsmen to insure themselves and their families against sickness and unemployment.

But almost from the beginning the growth of industrialisation produced its critics. By the 1820s and 1830s the heightened contrast between wealth and poverty was leading some to question the very foundations of the new society, and to propose, in the name either of Christian charity or social justice, fundamental reforms and new political systems.

18

Reformers and utopians

One of the most significant protests to develop from within the Church itself was the Liberal Catholic movement which began in France in 1829 under the leadership of the clerics Lamennais and Lacordaire with the support of the young peer, the Count of Montalembert. Totally opposed to the *ancien régime* and the control of the Church by the state, they urged through their journal *L'Avenir* freedom of conscience, of the press and education, the sovereignty of the people, universal suffrage and freedom of association. Considered dangerous to authority, the movement was condemned by the French government and by the pope in an encyclical of 1832. Nevertheless, the ideas survived and found expression in the work of a young student, Frederick Ozanam, who founded the Society of St Vincent de Paul for mutual aid and charity.

From outside the established order, and aiming at the overthrow of the capitalist sys-

tem as a whole, came a stream of socialist writings. Most of the early work was utopian and unrealistic, the product of the imagination of philosophers and intellectuals who were remote from practical politics, although their ideas contributed importantly to the later foundations of socialism.

One of the earliest was the Count of Saint-Simon (1760–1825), a ruined nobleman who became a violent critic of a social order based on competition and the exploitation of the most numerous class by a tiny minority of privileged owners. His conclusion was that it would be necessary to suppress this class, whose possessions and capital would thus revert to the state, the only legitimate owner. Society could then be reorganised, and new classes constructed on the basis of ability, not wealth.

In place of the power of Crown and Church there would be the power of the creative sections of the population—intellectuals, bankers, industrialists, workers—

Idealistic philosophy had its artistic counterpart in the Romantic Movement of writers, poets and painters.
Johann von Goethe (1749–1832) was the greatest genius in German literature. He is shown here (above) posed against a Roman landscape, in a portrait painted between 1786 and 1788 by Johann Heinrich Wilhelm Tischbein. Landscape painting became one of the leading characteristics of romanticism, reflecting the 'back-to-nature' attitude in revulsion against the artificiality of town life.
Right: The Sea of Ice at Mont Annert by Carl Ludwig Hackert.
Far right: romantic architecture and landscape—The Castle of Heidelberg in 1812 by George Auguste Wallis. (Goethemuseum, Frankfurt.)

all inspired by a common faith in service and progress.

Saint-Simon's influence was greater after his death than during his own lifetime. His *Memoirs* were not published until 1829. Two of his disciples, Enfantin and Bazard, tried to establish a small community in accordance with the principles of the master 'to each according to his ability, each man's ability to be judged by what he achieves,' but, like many similar ventures, the project failed because of internal disputes and a lawsuit brought by the state. Saint-Simon's significance lay in daring to challenge a system which, to nearly all men, had seemed God-given and eternal, and in the influence which his philosophy had on his contemporaries and successors.

Among these was the English socialist, Robert Owen (1771–1858), who conceived a society in which all power would belong to the working classes, organised into co-operative societies which would both own and control the instruments of production. The son of a draper, Owen had a successful career as an employer in the cotton industry

and then as manager of the largest cotton mills in Scotland, at New Lanark. It was during his time there as one of the few enlightened employers of the period that he developed his basic socialist principles : man is not good or evil by nature, but largely as a result of the environment in which he grows up ; and, secondly, that the machine is not something to be feared and destroyed, but to be encouraged for its power to lighten human labour and create vast new sources of wealth. However, to ensure that this wealth was fairly distributed among those who created it, Owen believed that the machine (including all the instruments of production) would need to be publicly owned and controlled, and taken out of the hands of private capitalists. These shattering views were published in his *New Moral View of Society* as early as 1813.

Although he had important effects on the development of management, education and co-operation, as a practical socialist Owen was no more successful than Saint-Simon's disciples. A socialist community in the United States, inappropriately named

'New Harmony', collapsed after a few years, and Owen's Grand National Consolidated Trade Union (1834), which was to have taken over British industry after a general strike, was defeated by the combined action of government and employers.

Similar ideas were developed by another French socialist, Fourier. The state was to disappear, and give place to self-governing socialist communities, each of about 2,000 people, which would be free associations in which all could devote themselves to the occupations of their choice, In this way, each would find personal fulfilment and happiness. Again, in the theory of Louis Blanc (1811–1882), all private industries would be incorporated into social workshops, where workers would choose their employers and share the profits. Proudhon (1809–1865) attacked the existence of private property ('property is theft'), the institutions of law and the state, even the sovereignty of the people ('universal suffrage is a lottery'). In his philosophy there was to be no system of government at all : he was the apostle of anarchy.

Writers and readers—the thirst for freedom of expression and education.
Above: portrait of Friedrich von Schiller, the celebrated German dramatist, poet and historian (1759–1805). His most popular play is Mary Stuart (1800). *This portrait is by Gerhard von Kugelgen. (Goethemuseum, Frankfurt.)*
Above right: A German reading room in 1850 by an anonymous artist. (Zeughaus, East Berlin.)
Far right: The poverty-stricken poet *by Karl Slitzweg. (Neue Pinakothek, Munich.)*
Right: portrait of Alfred de Musset, the French poet, playright and novelist. He is best remembered for his poetry, particularly his love lyrics. (Bibliothèque Nationale, Paris.)

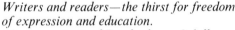

The very diversity of these views indicates that socialism was not, and could not be at this time, a political party with a well-defined programme. Its main theorists had been intellectuals and philosophers, often of aristocratic or middle-class background, remote from the hopes and aspirations of ordinary men. However, towards the end of the period socialism was to begin to pass from the scholar's study to the mines and factories, as reformers began to organise the working classes for more effective political action.

In Paris in 1836 the Federation of Just Men was founded by a group of emigré German revolutionaries, of whom a tailor, Weitling, was the leading figure. In 1847, at the Federation's annual congress in London, the name 'Communist League' was adopted. It was on this occasion that Karl Marx and Frederick Engels drew up the Communist Manifesto (published 1848) which was to prove the most influential political document of modern times.

The triumph of science

But to many contemporaries it was not so much the development of new political ideas or the artistic achievements of the Romantic Movement that characterised the age as the spectacular advances in scientific knowledge and application. The origins of the scientific revolution lay much further back in the seventeenth century, when men had first begun to observe, measure, analyse and deduce laws from the natural world around them, but at this time science was still part of philosophy the intellectual pursuit of gentlemen-scholars for its own intrinsic interest. By the nineteenth century scientific knowledge had come to provide the very basis of industrial and technological progress, the life-blood of the new age, no longer the pastime of gifted amateurs but the activity of professional scientists and research workers.

The new science rested fundamentally on basic mathematical theory, which was greatly advanced by a group of scholars from many countries. One of the characteristics of the new knowledge was that it did not observe national boundaries, but was developed by men of many countries, often working closely with each other by the exchange of ideas through meetings and publications. Thus Gauss, a professor at Göttingen University, did pioneer work in applying mathematical theory to electricity and magnetism; the Frenchman Monge

largely established descriptive geometry, while Laplace demonstrated the stability of the solar system. The Norwegian Abel worked on mathematical astronomy and Le Verrier, on the basis of pure calculation, discovered the existence of the planet Neptune which was only observed several years later by telescope.

Similar fundamental research was being pursued in physics which had developed little since its laws had been first established by Newton. Now, Biot and Arago made the first accurate measurements of the density of the air. Gay-Lussac discovered the laws of expansion of gas and Carnot defined the laws of thermodynamics (the science of the relations between heat and mechanical work) on which the Englishman James Joule later based his work.

Although these discoveries were the necessary basis for many new applications, their immediate contribution to human life and work sometimes seemed remote. Not so with the development of electricity which, from early in the century, began to be used for a variety of purposes. In 1800 the Italians Volta and Galvani constructed the first electric battery: within a few years discoveries by the Dane Oersted, the Frenchman Ampère, the Englishman Faraday and the German Ohm had defined the laws of electromagnetism, established the idea of induction and expounded the mathematics of electrical currents. By the 1840s the electric telegraph, invented by Morse and Steinheil, was in use in England, France and in some other countries.

Discoveries in one branch of science frequently led to developments in others. Electrolysis was used to isolate new chemical substances such as potassium, magnesium, sodium, chromium and aluminium, many of which were to have highly important industrial uses. Similarly, the discoveries in organic chemistry by Chevreul and Liebig led to the development of artificial fertilisers and to much new knowledge about the chemistry of food. Already at the beginning of the nineteenth century Dalton and Avogadro were outlining the first modern theories of atomic structure.

Biologists, meanwhile, were investigating the nature of the cell, the fundamental element in the tissues, which was discovered in 1830. Advances in medicine and, in particular, the discovery of anaesthetics, were beginning to make treatment and surgery safer and more practicable, though until after the middle of the century hospitals continued to be places in which patients often died of diseases other than those with which they entered.

More fundamental research still was being undertaken into the nature of the earth itself. Detailed study of rocks enabled geologists to reconstruct the principal stages in the evolution of the earth's crust, while the examination of fossils by Cuvier laid the foundations of the science of palaeontology.

Right: romantic art. The Nightmare *by Henri Fuseli (1741–1825), the Anglo-Swiss painter. (Goethemuseum, Frankfurt.)*
After 1815 the British Empire underwent unprecedented expansion, much of it by acquisition from France at the end of the Napoleonic Wars.
Far right: the British commander, Arthur Wellesley, Duke of Wellington, surrounded by his general staff. He entered the army in 1787 and rose rapidly in rank, assuming command of the British, Portuguese and Spanish forces on the Iberian peninsula during the campaign against Napoleon. His greatest triumph was at Waterloo in 1815 when, aided by the Prussians under Blücher, he won one of the most decisive battles in history. (Bibliothèque Nationale, Paris.)

From here it was a short step to the posing of questions about the origins of man. Some of Cuvier's pupils remained convinced of the unchanging nature of species since their original creation, yet, to others, the discoveries of fossil remains, some of them closely similar to *homo sapiens* seemed to argue some kind of evolutionary process from which modern man had developed. Why had some prehistoric animals disappeared from the earth while others had survived in changed, though recognisable form? Lamarck and Saint-Hilaire suggested a theory of evolution of species under the impact of changes in heredity and environment, upon which Charles Darwin was later to build. Such views were, of course, irreconcilable with the teachings of the Christian church about the special creation of man, and opened a long controversy between science and religion.

But the spirit of scientific enquiry was not confined to the exploration of matter. To many people in the early nineteenth century science was all-important and all-embracing a tool that could unlock all doors and expose all secrets. Scientific method could be applied to history, to the civilisations of the past, as readily as it could to physics or chemistry. It was in this spirit that Champollion deciphered the meaning of hiero-glyphics, and thus founded the study of Egyptology, while excavations in Greece and Mesopotamia began the modern study of archaeology. It was this profound belief in the power of science that gave to the age so much of its confidence, its sense of purpose and inevitability of progress.

The romantic age

Running parallel with the scientific movement of the day, in some ways complementary but in others contradictory to it, was the romantic movement. Its origins lay in the violent upheavals of revolutionary France and the Napoleonic era, which gave rise to changes in the ways of life, attitudes, tastes and feelings of a whole generation.

Napoleon had been ultimately defeated by the traditional monarchies and aristocracies of Europe, and romanticism found its first expression in writers wishing to affirm their anti-revolutionary faith. Romanticism was a philosophy of protest against prevailing circumstances, changing as the circumstances changed. Thus, the early writings of the exiled Chateaubriand showed a fiercely conservative outlook, and both the young Alfred de Vigny and Victor Hugo proclaimed themselves fervent monarchists. It was natural that among subject peoples conquered by the sword of France, writers and poets should make themselves the champions of national feeling. They were anxious to assert their difference and individuality, to demonstrate their own distinct culture, language and literature. To oppressed peoples, history is a lifeline and a bulwark against the destruction of a nation's individuality.

But after 1815, the re-establishment of conservative monarchies throughout Europe and the absolutist policies of the Holy Alliance no longer satisfied romantic spirits eager for personal liberty and freedom. Some, like Victor Hugo, returned to the liberal camp and the literature of protest. Others retreated from the real world into a world of nature that had never been, endowed with sublime beauty, solitude and melancholy. The Germany of Goethe and Schiller was the principal home of literary romanticism, but England was also brilliantly represented by the poets Coleridge, Byron, Shelley and Keats and the historical works of Sir Walter Scott. Young people in many countries were fired with enthusiasm for the supposedly Celtic poems of the ancient bard Ossian—in fact, written by a Scotsman, Macpherson, about 1760—and Lamartine could write 'Ossian was the Homer of my early years'. Romantics, no

less than modern artists, were not uncommonly subject to self-deception.

In many European countries, however, romantics constituted an uninfluential minority desperately seeking to express their views against strongly entrenched, classical schools of literature. In France particularly they had to struggle to get their works published or produced on the stage, as did Lermontov against the forces of reaction in Russia. In such countries, where absolutist regimes had been re-established after the overthrow of Napoleon, romantics tended to be regarded as near revolutionaries, troublemakers, purveyors of anti-government literature, opponents of order, authority and religion. Some, it is true, were no more than wayward, angry young men, a few were wicked or depraved. But the death of Byron at Missolonghi, fighting for the independence of Greece against the despotic Turk, and the premature end of Lermontov, killed in a duel, symbolised the generous ideals, the courage and selflessness of the romantic spirit at its best. Such ideals were to find different, more positive outlets in the revolutions of 1830 and 1848.

England after Waterloo

In 1815 England came triumphantly to the end of a war in which she had been involved almost continuously for twenty-two years. In a real sense it was her victory. Although at the end, at Waterloo, the English armies had done little more than hold the line until the arrival of Blücher and the Prussians, England had been at the centre of the coalitions which ultimately defeated Napoleon and had provided the money and the war materials on which the armies were raised. Above all she had kept the seaways open and free from French domination. But victory had not been gained lightly. The long war left a crippling debt, an economy that had been subject to violent fluctuations and a working population which had been denied many freedoms in order that the enslaved of Europe should be freed. In some respects, the postwar difficulties and hardships were more acute than the wartime ones had been.

Parliamentary aristocracy

The England of 1815 remained, socially and politically at least, essentially the England of the eighteenth century. Despite the Industrial Revolution, which was rapidly changing the basis of Britain's economic wealth from land to industry and trade, all real power still remained in the hands of a territorial aristocracy numbering no more than a few thousand families. They represented the view—once arguable but by now irrelevant—that those who owned the land of Britain should control its destinies and public affairs. Since the 'Glorious Revolution' of 1688 Britain's system of government had been a parliamentary monarchy, with effective control of national policies in the hands of the two Houses of Parliament rather than the crown. The power of the monarchy had since been further reduced by the insanity of George III and the emergence of powerful parliamentary leaders like Chatham and Pitt. The peers of the realm had hereditary seats in the House of Lords where, together with the lords spiritual, they formed a solid bulwark not only against revolution but against reform. Although most legislation was now initiated in the lower chamber, the lords could always reject, delay or amend it out of recognition. In local affairs they also wielded immense influence through their appointment to the magistracy and county administration: their control of local justice and the administration of poor relief could be relied on to ensure a docile, even servile, rural population.

The Bank of England was the only bank in the world whose notes were accepted everywhere as the equivalent of gold. Through institutions like this, Lloyd's great insurance house and the numerous exchanges for metals and other raw materials, Britain became the centre of the world's money and finance market. After the French defeat in 1815 Louis XVIII had to pay France's war debts into a private English bank.
Above: Lloyd's—insurance brokers to the world.
Above right: Leadenhall Market, one of the great London exchanges. (Bibliothèque Nationale, Paris.)

In theory the House of Commons, with members elected by the counties and boroughs of the four kingdoms, was a more representative body. But here, too, the right to vote and the right to election of a member rested on a property qualification which enfranchised a mere 150,000 out of a population of more than 15,000,000. Once flourishing centres such as the ancient port of Aldeborough in Suffolk still sent more than one representive to the Commons even though they were now reduced to small villages or hamlets (in Aldeborough's case through coastal erosion sinking the city beneath the sea). In many 'pocket' and 'rotten' boroughs electors were sufficiently few for their votes to be bought or commanded, and it was common practice for wealthy young men seeking a political career to buy a parliamentary seat at a price of £5–6,000. Of 658 seats in the Commons only about fifty were actually fought by rival candidates.

By no stretch of imagination, then, could Britain's parliamentary system in 1815 be described as democratic. The privileged members of both Houses divided themselves between the two great parties, Whigs and Tories, the differences between which were by now all but lost in history. Originally, Tories had stood for the rights of the Crown and the Anglican Church, Whigs for parliamentary government, freedom of conscience and moderate reform. But both parties consisted of landowners equally devoted to the maintenance of the existing class structure and equally remote from the new centres of power that were beginning to reshape English society.

The two Englands

England in 1815 presented a strange contrast of the old and the new. In the countryside, where more than two-thirds of the population still lived, there was much that was traditional and unchanging: ways of life, methods of agriculture, food, dress and habits were still almost medieval, especially in the remoter parts of the West and North.

But, by contrast, in the Midlands, Lancashire and Yorkshire industrialisation had made rapid progress during the wars, spurred on by the demand for guns and munitions, ships, clothing and army supplies of all kinds. Vast new centres of population sprang up as rural dwellers were attracted by the opportunities and earnings of industry. Within the first half of the century Birmingham trebled in size, Manchester quadrupled, Bradford increased no less than eight-fold. This rapid and unplanned growth of cities created immense problems—of accommodation, sanitation, local government and recreation—whose solution lay far in the future. More immediately, it showed up the inadequacies and inequalities of a parliamentary system which gave two seats to a 'rotten borough' of a score of voters but denied representation to a great new city like Manchester.

But in one respect, at least, England had an advantage over other European countries. Here there was no impassable gulf between the aristocracy of birth and the aristocracy of wealth: the two met and mingled, their sons were educated together in the public schools, their families not infrequently intermarried. Robert Peel, the son of a successful Lancashire cotton manufacturer, could become an M.P. at twenty-one and, ultimately, Prime Minister; Richard Arkwright, the wandering barber who invented (some said stole) the idea of a water-powered spinning frame could be knighted and created lord-lieutenant of the county of Nottinghamshire, an office usually reserved for a territorial lord. Industrialisation offered to some glittering prizes of wealth and social mobility unknown to previous ages. To others, perhaps a majority of the population, it offered misery heightened by the evidence of wealth about them.

The postwar depression

At the end of the war England entered upon a long depression which brought to many even greater hardship than the war had done. Industries lay depressed with the sudden cessation of wartime demand, agriculture no longer enjoyed the protection that Napoleon's blockade had brought and began to contract, while European countries, impoverished after years of conquest and exploitation, could not afford to resume their former level of trade. It was, in fact, twenty years after 1815 before British exports recovered to their previous level. Added to the existing problems of unemployment and low wages were some half a million demobilised soldiers and sailors, suddenly thrown on to a labour market that could not absorb them. The years from 1815 to 1820 were among the darkest in English history when many feared, with some cause, a repetition of the events which had torn France apart in 1789.

Radicalism—an extreme form of politics which advocated fundamental reform of the constitutional and financial system—grew to brief importance under such popular leaders as Cobbett and Hunt. In their hatred of industrialisation they preached a naive

Old and new industries. Despite the progress
of the Industrial Revolution much industry
in the first half of the nineteenth century
remained small-scale, dependent on the skill
of the worker.
Far left above: coining money in the early
nineteenth century.
Far left below: King William IV (1830–
1837), third son of George III. Never
popular with his people, William spent much
of his life connected with the British Navy.
Centre left: a workshop for printing
postage stamps.
Top: the great gaming room at Brook's,
St James's Street, London.
Above left: a watch-house, forerunner of
the police station.
Above: Daniel O'Connell, founder of
the movement for Irish Home Rule. In 1843
O'Connell was imprisoned for encouraging
political discontent, but he was released by
the House of Lords. He is credited with
creating national unity in Ireland.
Left: the reading room of the Royal
Institution of Great Britain. Founded in
1799, its aim was to promote science and
the extension of useful knowledge.
(Bibliothèque Nationale, Paris.)

'back-to-the-land' philosophy which seemed attractive to populations of former peasants exposed to the insecurities of town life. Significantly, the cause of the 'Peterloo Massacre' in Manchester in 1819, when a defenceless crowd was charged by squadrons of cavalry, was a speech by Hunt, not on the problem of wages or unemployment, but on the subject of land reform.

Most labour movements in the first half of the century had this strong agrarian background. A majority of the new town dwellers were peasants by origin, unaccustomed to the regularity of factory work and the overcrowded life in slums and tenements. They turned instinctively to solutions that offered simpler, better understood relationships in which men seemed to be something more than mere instruments of production. Working people gave their support to Radicalism, not because they understood or even cared very much about abstract democratic principles but because it represented a protest against the unacceptable conditions of life. To its few middle- and upper-class supporters it was much more—a progressive, democratic demand for a government responsible to the popular will and an administrative system based on efficiency rather than privilege.

To such suggestions the governments of the day responded with severe repression. The Tory party remained in office from the end of the war until 1830, first under Lord Liverpool, later under the wartime hero, the Duke of Wellington. Their belief was that the British constitution was perfect and that any attempt to disturb it must be put down firmly. Trade Unions were illegal until 1824 and even after that striking was still a criminal offence, public meetings and meeting-places required to be licensed and newspapers were subject to a crippling stamp duty of five pence a copy. Together with such measures went a crude system which paid a meagre dole to labourers whose earnings were inadequate to support their families (the Speenhamland System of poor relief) and which had the effect of impoverishing whole areas of the country.

Scandals at court

In 1820 the mad George III was succeeded by his son, the former prince regent, who had been notorious as a beau and a rake. For many years now he had deserted his wife, Caroline of Brunswick, in favour of a succession of mistresses. Caroline had finally left England in 1814 to live abroad, and George, the regent, had appointed a commission to investigate her conduct. Its report appeared in 1819, full of supposedly scandalous revelations about the intimate life of the Princess Caroline. She, however, refused to be divorced, and published an open letter defending her own conduct and attacking that of George. In June 1820 she set sail for

The accession of Queen Victoria to the throne in 1837 transformed the relationship between the crown and the people.
Above left: a portrait, painted in 1843 by Winterhalter, of the young Victoria wearing the Order of the Garter. Victoria was the *daughter of Edward, duke of Kent (fourth son of George III) and Victoria of Saxe-Coburg. (Musée de Versailles.)*
Below: the coronation procession, 1837.
Right: the changing of the Horse Guards in 1844. (Bibliothèque Nationale, Paris.)

25 Januar.   8 Februar.

England to be crowned alongside her husband.

On her progress to London, and in the capital, Caroline was received by enthusiastic crowds who saw her as a wronged and innocent victim of a degenerate king. Divorce proceedings opened at Westminster in July, and the private lives of the British monarchy were exposed to the tales of lackeys and ladies-in-waiting. Public regard for the Crown had not been at a lower ebb since the Civil War of the seventeenth century, and there were many who predicted a republican future for the country which had developed the concept of constitutional monarchy. The court was unable to reach a decision, but ultimately Caroline was induced to yield by the payment of a handsome pension: one of the most ugly chapters in the English monarchy closed with an unseemly bribe.

The post-war depression and public disorder of the period 1815–20 had shown up the inadequacies—indeed, irrelevancies—of both political parties to the changing needs of the time. But after 1824 Tory policies began to receive a new direction at the hands of a group of enlightened young politicians —Canning at the Foreign Office, Peel at the Home Office and Huskisson at the Board of Trade—who appreciated the necessity of reshaping policies in the light of Britain's changing economic conditions and world role.

Middle-class reform

'Enlightened Toryism', which Sir Robert Peel was later to develop into the new Conservative Party, gave the government a fresh lease of life. Its appeal was particularly to the rising class of merchants and industrialists, who were favoured by reductions in the tariff system and by modifications to the Corn Laws. Under the Corn Law of 1815, passed in response to pressure by the landed interest, the import of foreign wheat was totally prohibited when the English price was less than eighty shillings a quarter. Whether it had very much effect on the price of wheat is debatable, but it certainly acted to the disadvantage of exporters who wished to sell to countries like Germany, Hungary and Russia who had little else but wheat to offer in exchange. The Corn Laws therefore constituted a serious hindrance to the expansion of world trade, from which Britain, as the greatest exporting nation, suffered particularly. By various acts in the later 1820s a sliding scale was substituted for the total prohibition, so that duties on imported wheat remained high when the English price was low, and vice versa. These measures at least opened the way for the ultimate repeal of the Corn Laws in 1846.

Other reforms by the enlightened Tories were of benefit to the population as a whole. Peel, as home secretary, began to modernise the penal system by abolishing the death sentence on several hundreds of petty offences. At the same time, his establishment of the Metropolitan Police made the detection and punishment of crime more effective. In 1828 the Test Acts, which had debarred Nonconformists from the holding of public office as M.P.s, magistrates, etc., were repealed and, more significant still, Catholic emancipation was passed in the next year. This issue was forced by the 'election' of the Irish Catholic leader, Daniel O'Connell, for County Clare, and rather than face what might have been a civil war in Ireland the prime minister, Wellington, acceded to the demands of Catholics to be treated as equal citizens. After more than two centuries of persecution religious toleration was finally established in Britain.

'She was conscious', said someone close to Queen Victoria, 'of a marvellous and mysterious duty imposed by providence.' The queen herself believed that a mere woman was unfit to discharge the function of the monarch.
Left: the queen visits Prince Frederick William of Prussia in Berlin in 1858. The procession is passing under the Brandenburg Gate. (Kunstbibliothek, West Berlin.)
Right: Louis Philippe, king of France, escorts Queen Victoria and Prince Albert aboard the royal yacht at Tréport in 1843. Painted by Eugène Isabey. (Musée de Versailles.)
Below: an evening at the New Covent Garden Theatre. The original theatre was burnt down in 1808 and again in 1856. It was rebuilt in 1858 to house ballet and opera. (Bibliothèque Nationale, Paris.)

The Great Reform Bill of 1832

Catholic emancipation did not solve the problem of Ireland. Tenants of English landlords, forced to pay tithes to the English Church and subjected by the Act of Union of 1800 to English political domination, the Irish now laid claims to absolute independence.

O'Connell and his Young Ireland party renewed their agitation. Monster demonstrations were organised, particularly between 1843 and 1847, and there was even an abortive attempt at revolution in 1848. But Ireland was crushed by poverty and exhausted by famine. In 1846 the potato crop on which the majority of the population depended, was hit by blight, and thousands starved to death. Between 1841 and 1851 a million Irish—many of them the most intelligent and resourceful part of the population—emigrated to England and America. For the time being political issues were merged in national calamity.

Meanwhile, in England, agitation for parliamentary reform had been growing with an uneasy alliance between Whigs, Philosophical Radicals and some sections of the working classes. In 1830 the hated George IV died and was succeeded by

William IV, of no great intelligence though more amenable. Revolutions in France and Belgium had some influence in England: in 1830–31 there was a large-scale rising of agricultural labourers throughout the eastern and southern counties demanding higher wages, fairer rents and an improved system of poor relief. Events were converging towards a major political change.

In the general election of 1830 the Whigs were returned to power under Lord Grey. Their first act was to introduce a measure for parliamentary reform, which passed into law in 1832 only after numerous amendments and an initial rejection in the House of Lords. Although always known as the 'Great Reform Bill' its provisions were modest enough, and far less than the Radicals had hoped. It abolished the separate representation of small towns with less than 2,000 inhabitants, and left towns with 2,000–4,000 with only one member; 143 seats were then available for distribution among the great new cities and among those counties which were not adequately represented.

Manchester and Birmingham for the first time received their own members of parliament, but even after 1832 an ancient borough of 2,010 inhabitants could still return its own representative. The other main provision of the Act was the extension of the franchise to householders in the towns rated at £10 a year and to £50 a year tenant farmers in the country—essentially the urban and rural middle classes: the electorate was thus increased to 600,000 voters. The Act did not enfranchise the working classes, nor make voting secret. Parliamentary participation was still to rest on the possession of property as an indication of worth and responsibility. The Reform Act in no way converted England into a democracy, though it was the first, and in some ways the decisive step in that process.

The new poor law

The next task of the Whig government after the reform of parliament was reform of the poor law. A system which paid a dole to all and sundry, which encouraged the idle and discouraged the diligent, and which acted as a deterrent to labour mobility, was totally unacceptable to the 'practical' principles which inspired middle-class Whigs. In 1832 a Royal Commission, headed by the great classical economist Nassau Senior and the lawyer Edwin Chadwick, was appointed to investigate the existing provisions for the poor and to make recommendations for their reform.

Senior accepted the pessimistic view of the Reverend Thomas Malthus that population would inevitably outstrip the resources necessary to feed it unless kept down by 'natural checks'. Poverty was inherent in society, but pauperism could be eradicated by suitably stringent forms of relief. Under the Poor Law Amendment Act of 1834 the

Britain's remarkable industrial progress in the nineteenth century earned her the title of 'the workshop of the world'. Technological progress was now concentrated on iron and steel, engineering, shipbuilding and railway construction. By the 1870s Britain produced two-thirds of the world's coal, half the world's textiles, and accounted for one-third of world trade.
Above: a modern engineering factory of 1850. (Bibliothèque Nationale, Paris.)

payment of doles, at least to those fit to work, was to cease: in future, the only form of relief would be in workhouses where conditions would deliberately be made 'less eligible' (i.e. more unpleasant) than those of the poorest paid free workers. Here, husbands and wives would be separated, fed on the sparsest diet and made to labour at the most uncongenial tasks. Behind the outward cruelty, however, there lay the hope that these measures would force up the level of wages, make labour more mobile and, not least, bring down the cost of poor relief. In this last respect the act was a marked success. As Carlyle commented cynically, 'If paupers are made miserable, paupers must needs decline in multitude. It is a secret known to all rat catchers'.

In a broad sense, the Amendment Act was in tune with the general philosophy of the Whigs of removing antiquated restrictions and bringing about greater freedom. The Municipal Corporations Act of 1835 reconstituted the local government of boroughs, establishing elected councils in all towns above the size of 25,000 inhabitants. More important, an Act of 1833 abolished slavery in the British Empire, so completing the work begun by Wilberforce who had earlier succeeded in stopping the slave trade in 1807. In the same year, 1833, the great East India Company was deprived of its monopoly of trading with the East, and the gateway thus opened for a remarkable expansion of British trade in India, China and Japan. All these measures were, in effect, advancing the cause of Free Trade, which became the guiding philosophy—almost the religion—of the Liberal Party later in the century.

The beginning of the Victorian Age

William IV died in 1837, to more or less universal indifference. England remained a monarchy, but for more than a century the English people had had no feeling for their kings except amusement or contempt. A young girl of eighteen was now to regain the affection and respect that kings had forfeited.

For nearly three-quarters of a century (1837–1901) Victoria was to unite the people and the monarchy in an intimate, almost mysterious, relationship. Although she came to learn her position as a constitutional monarch very well and did not, after the first few years, attempt to intervene in party political issues, she was often able to represent the views and interests of the people to the government, and hence to play an important part in the shaping of policy. In her simple, naive way she exercised a moral, moderating influence on politics, restraining the hotheaded, encouraging the timid and the humane, steadfastly opposing repression either at home or abroad.

Victoria had been a highly unlikely successor to the throne of England. The problem

had presented itself during the long lifetime of George III, when the royal family comprised seven princes, two of whom succeeded as George IV and William IV. But none of them had any children—at least, any legitimate children capable of succeeding to the throne. The Duke of Kent, who was deep in debt, agreed 'in the interests of the kingdom' to contract a 'reasonable' marriage. He left his mistress to marry a German princess, Victoria of Leiningen, a member of the distinguished Saxe-Coburg family. Of this union Victoria was born in May 1819.

The future queen was brought up strictly, seriously, even humbly for a person of her rank. At eighteen, she was intellectually unprepared for her role, though imbued with devotion to her task and a deep desire to raise the status of the monarchy from the ignominy of previous reigns. Political intrigue developed early around the young queen whom every politician thought to influence, but Victoria acted mainly on the counsel of Lord Melbourne, the Whig prime minister after 1834, who offered wise and palatable advice on English constitutional practice. Victoria's marriage to her cousin, Prince Albert of Saxe-Coburg, also added strength, intelligence and moral purpose to the new monarchy.

In some important respects, the long reign of Victoria instituted a new kind of monarchy which was one of the many adaptations that nineteenth-century England was obliged to make. Monarchy in the past had been associated with rural England, with the territorial aristocracy and the 'gentlemanly' pursuits of farming, sport, 'the season' and leisure. Such a role would have been impossible for the queen anyway, but, particularly through her husband, she chose to identify herself much more with urban and industrial interests, with the new sources of activity and wealth that were transforming England into a middle-class society. The royal court was still as magnificent as ever, there were still rural retreats in Scotland and the Isle of Wight (no longer Brighton), but the energy and moral purpose, the devotion to work and good causes, of the royal couple were new characteristics of the monarchy, closely in tune with the principles of bourgeois life. The queen's unsophisticated taste in literature, music and interior decoration was mirrored in thousands of suburban homes, and the extensive yet virtuous domestic life of the monarchy served to set a seal on the Victorian preoccupation with family, hearth and home.

The reshaping of the monarchy to essentially middle-class standards and ideals was only one of many adaptations that English institutions had to made in response to economic and social changes. By the 1870s complete free trade had been established except for a few duties kept for revenue purposes only. Recruitment to the expanded Civil Service had been established on competitive principles in place of privilege. The

powers of local authorities had been enlarged to include responsibility for public health and, in part at least, for housing. More important still, in 1870 the state reluctantly accepted a duty towards popular education by instituting a system of public elementary schools. Although the composition of parliament was still unrepresentative of the changes taking place outside it, even here the beginnings of a modern party system were discernible, with stronger party discipline and greater concentration of authority in the hands of the cabinet. This development became marked only later during the great ministries of Gladstone and Disraeli.

The other nation

The middle classes had made substantial gains in the early years of the queen's reign. But Victorian prosperity rested on a wide substructure of poverty in the working classes, for whom it must often have seemed that England had nothing to offer except unending toil, a slum dwelling and a pauper's

grave. After the Reform Act of 1832 the radical alliance with the middle classes collapsed; the workers were still unenfranchised and unrepresented, and felt betrayed by those to whom they had lent support. Now there seemed no one to take their cause.

The saddest plight of all was that of the factory children, forced to work at the age of six or seven from five in the morning until seven or eight at night. Many were too exhausted to eat, some were maimed and even killed by the machines they tended. Industrialisation in its early stages required cheap, amenable labour, and women and children could often perform the routine tasks it demanded with little or no training.

Direct political action by the working classes had, for the time being, been tried and had failed. Some improvements were to come, however, from philanthropists and humanitarians concerned for the sufferings of the poor, and especially for the welfare of children. Lord Shaftesbury was particularly successful in compelling the investigation of conditions in factories and coal mines, which

formed the necessary basis for the legislative control of employment which began in the Factory Act of 1833.

Robert Owen had already demonstrated at the New Lanark Mills, contrary to all popular belief, that humane factory management could reduce hours of work, pay higher wages, and still make handsome profits. As an enlightened capitalist employer Owen was an outstanding success, as a socialist philosopher and educational theorist brilliant and inspiring, as a practical political leader an utter failure. His schemes for co-operative production and, more ambitious still, for the Grand National Consolidated Trade Union (1833–4) which was to have 'nationalised' British industry and run it socialistically, collapsed under the united attack of government and employers. The enduring memorial to Robert Owen, symbolic alike of his inspiration and failure, is the case of the Tolpuddle Martyrs (1834), sentenced to seven years transportation for having dared to form a trade union.

Begun in the middle of the eighteenth
century, the conquest of India was
completed a century later with the
occupation of the Punjab. India was to
become a huge market for British textiles
and Britain's main source of tea and other
luxury imports.
Above: shipping in the West India Dock,
London.
Right: Indian soldiers in the British army
in India. (Bibliothèque Nationale, Paris.)

The expansion of the British Empire was often achieved only after difficult and bloody conquest.
Above right: a charge by dragoons at the battle of Sobraon, 1846. In 1857 the Indian garrisons rebelled. Soldiers had been punished because they had refused to use a new kind of cartridge said to be greased with the fat of cows and pigs. The handling of these cartridges would have caused a breach of Hindu and Muslim law.
Right: the attack on Lucknow, 1858.
Far right: The 52nd Infantry force the Kashmir Gate at Delhi in 1857.
(Bibliothèque Nationale, Paris.)

The Chartist challenge

The failure of Owen's schemes for a socialist millennium was to revive the agitation for direct political representation. The lawsuits which had struck at the trades unions, the harshness of the new Poor Law and the limited success of the Factory Act of 1833 all served to indicate to the worker that legislative policy would continue to be made regardless of his interests so long as he continued to be excluded from parliament.

In 1836 the London Working Men's Association was formed to campaign for parliamentary representation. It was, in itself, a moderate movement of working-class intelligentsia, deriving much of its programme from late eighteenth-century radicalism, but it quickly became caught up in much more violent agitations in the Midlands and North, particularly against the new workhouse 'bastilles'. In 1837 'The People's Charter' was formulated—a demand for six democratic reforms the most important of which were manhood suffrage, secret voting and the payment of members of parliament.

Chartism was the major working class movement of the first half of the century, dominating the stage from 1837 until 1848. Although outwardly a political movement, seeking to persuade parliament of the justness of its demands by the presentation of monster petitions, its root cause were economic and social discontent, and its main support came in the two major periods of depression and unemployment, 1839–42 and 1847–8. As one of its leaders, Joseph Stephens, put it, 'Chartism was a bread and cheese question, a knife and fork question'. Its appeal, especially after 'physical force' leaders like Feargus O'Connor took over command from those who advocated only moral persuasion, was to the hungry and destitute, the unemployed and the underemployed, the sweated workers and the casualties of industrialisation.

Petitions presented in 1839 and 1842 were unheeded by parliament. The last, of 1848, which purported to contain six million signatures, was examined and found to include less than two million, many pages in the same hand and including such unlikely supporters as the Duke of Wellington and Mr Punch. The charter was laughed out of existence in an atmosphere of near hysterical relief.

Chartism failed for many reasons—because its aims were over-ambitious, because it was badly led, lacked funds and influence, but, not least, because it was firmly opposed by the ruling classes who alone might have championed it in parliament. Nevertheless, it has rightly been regarded as the first mass movement of an identifiable working class, and its very existence helped to draw attention to what Disraeli called 'The Condition of England Question', Gradually a social conscience was aroused on specific evils, which found expression in legislation regulating the hours and conditions in factories and mines, the removal of street refuse, the conduct of common lodging houses and the adulteration of food and drugs.

In general, however, the mood of the mid-century was one of unbounded optimism and confidence in Britain's progress. After the depression of 1848 England seemed to move on to a new plateau of prosperity which began to bring gains, not only to the employing class, but to all sections of the community. The 'Golden Age', if it had not already dawned, was imminent.

The triumph of free trade

Britain's economic success in the middle of the century was due in no small part to her adoption of a policy of Free Trade. It fell, ironically, to the lot of Peel, the leader of the Conservative Party from 1841 to 1846, to initiate the process by abandoning the Corn Laws in 1846. By so doing he acted against the wishes of the landed gentry which had helped to vote him into office, and left his party split and in the wilderness.

Peel had become gradually convinced of the necessity for a free trade in corn, partly

as a social reform which could cheapen the cost of bread to the working classes, partly as an economic measure which would enable Britain to sell more manufactured goods to countries which could only pay in food and raw materials. These and other arguments had been forcibly put by the Anti-Corn Law League under its founder, Richard Cobden, a Manchester industrialist of humble origins who had made a fortune in the cotton trade. The success of the League was in direct contrast to the failure of Chartism. It was efficiently organised and well led; it had the support of the middle classes and of many M.P.s it used methods of propaganda such as the distribution of millions of pamphlets through the new penny post to ensure that its message was heard throughout the land. The campaign was a masterpiece of persuasion, essentially modern in its use of the mass media and its deliberate enlistment of influential support.

It seems that Peel had been convinced of the necessity for total removal of the Corn Laws by 1842 or 1843, and that thereafter he was only awaiting the right occasion. This came in 1846, with the Irish Famine, when thousands more would have died if the free import of wheat had not been allowed. Repeal was carried through parliament by a minority of the government (the 'Peelites') with the support of the Whigs, and against the bitter opposition of the landowning Tories. It opened the way for the establishment of complete freedom of trade in the next decade.

By sponsoring repeal of the Corn Laws Peel split his party and committed political suicide. The young Disraeli made his reputation at this moment by denouncing his leader as a betrayer, and putting himself at the head of the protectionist Tories. Gradually he welded a new Conservative party out of the ruins, dedicated to social reform at home and expansion of the empire abroad. 'Peelites' ultimately amalgamated with some of the Whigs to form the new Liberal party, of which Gladstone, the natural heir and successor of Peel, was to become the leader. Liberalism stood, above all, for Free Trade and free enterprise, for democratic reform and for a policy of peace abroad. These two great leaders were to dominate British politics almost until the end of the century.

The British Empire

With the War of American Independence (1776–83) the first British Empire had come to an end. But during the nineteenth century a second British Empire was constructed partly by acquisition, partly by conquest, partly by treaty, which was greater than the first—greater, indeed, than the world had ever seen—which was at once her pride and the envy of other nations. Much of it had come by conquest at the expense of France and her allies, Spain and Holland, during the Revolutionary and Napoleonic Wars—huge areas in India and Canada, Ceylon and the Cape of Good Hope, many of the West Indian islands and strategic possessions in the Mediterranean like Gibraltar, Malta and the Ionian Isles. But there was little deliberate plan about the development of the empire—it has even been said that it was born 'in a fit of absence of mind'. A large empire, and the ability to maintain it and the sea routes between it, was a symbol of the power and status of the mother country. Some territories supplied useful products and raw materials, some provided substantial outlets for British manufactures, but in general the second British Empire came into being not so much from economic or military reasons but rather because of a rather ill-defined pride of possession often combined with genuine religious and humanitarian impulses.

British India

The special pride of the Victorian Empire was India. By the end of the Napoleonic War Britain was firmly established in the territories of the Ganges and of the Deccan

39

in the south, but did not yet hold the whole sub-continent. The struggle against the Mahratta chiefs (1817), the conquest of the territories round the Indus and the war against the savage Sikhs of the Punjab occupied the first half of the nineteenth century. Then followed the task of governing and administering these vast dominions, a task accomplished on the whole with efficiency and honesty by the Indian Army and the Indian Civil Service, reconstituted on modern lines even before the reforms in home administration. For many functions the East India Company continued to act as the agent of the British government until 1853.

Protection of sea routes also assumed a major importance in the far-flung British Empire. St Helena, the Cape of Good Hope, Mauritius, Aden (acquired 1839), Ceylon and Singapore (1819) all became impregnable bastions and barriers to the colonial ambitions of other European powers.

Elsewhere, where outright conquest failed or seemed too costly, Britain contented herself with establishing a protective belt around her dominions. After the failure of the conquest of Afghanistan in 1842, the British army confined itself to fortifying the mountain passes of the North-West Frontier. To the north of India the Himalayas provided a natural barrier capable of repelling any invader, while to the north-east Burma was at least partly occupied after two campaigns in 1826 and 1852.

India also served as a base for the domination of the Far East. The old East India Company had always claimed the monopoly of trade with all lands east of the Cape of Good Hope, though its success had been virtually confined to the mainland of India. Now, the search for ever wider markets was to open up the formerly closed countries of the Far East which had for centuries sought to insulate themselves against the influence of the West. The Opium War of 1840-2 forced China to open five ports to British trade, including the great cities of Canton and Shanghai, and to cede the island of Hong Kong, a trading centre and strategic port in the Pacific. In 1857 trade was opened with Siam, and in 1858 with Japan.

The white empire

In India and the Far East the motives of imperialism were economic and military, sometimes religious and philanthropic. It was never intended that British people should settle permanently in tropical and subtropical latitudes, where they were exposed to a harsh climate, endemic diseases and sudden, even violent, death. Countries which were so inhospitable, poor and already over populated, offered little attraction to the English emigrant.

On the other hand, the mother country herself seemed to offer few prospects of health and happiness to many of those who

laboured in the early days of industrialisation, and there were parts of the empire—South Africa, Australia, New Zealand and Canada—where the climate was acceptable, where farmland could be had cheaply or even free, and where a man of energy and purpose could be master of his own destiny. There was a steady and continuous stream of emigrants from Britain, amounting, during the course of the century, to no less than twenty million people. Britain's human export, many of them men and women of above average intelligence and initiative, was perhaps her most important and enduring gift to the world.

To many, the Cape of Good Hope, acquired from Holland in 1815, seemed to offer the most attractive prospects. The original Dutch settlers, the Boers, were gradually pushed further back into the interior as more settlers arrived from Britain. Isolated and unprotected, they were unable to oppose the abolition of slavery in 1833, though this threatened to deprive them of the black labour force on which their agricultural economy depended.

In 1833 the Great Trek took the Boers

Below: British emissaries announce the treaty of 20 December 1815, by which the trade in Negroes was abolished. (Bibliothèque Nationale, Paris.)

from one side of the river Vaal to the other, into Natal. When this was annexed by Britain in 1844, the Boers trekked again, and Britain now recognised as independent the Republics of Transvaal and The Orange Free State. For the time being the issue seemed to be resolved—the diamond mines had not yet been discovered.

At the other end of the world Australia, remote and open, seemed less attractive to settlers, and until the middle of the century was used primarily as a convict settlement. But the success of many ex-prisoners as sheep farmers, the availability of free land, and the discovery of gold in 1851 soon began to exert a magnetic effect on emigrants. Rich lands also awaited the settler in New Zealand, where the warlike Maoris were defeated and pushed back into the hills. In Canada, especially in the state of Quebec, the situation was different. Here, English colonists encountered an existing white population of French descent, hostile to British domination and acutely aware of their distinct origins and culture. Little by little the French were swamped by continued migration, though they continued jealously to preserve their own customs and ways of life.

Origins of the Commonwealth

The spread of the 'white empire' posed new problems for the home government. The 'black' colonies, it was argued, constituted an 'empire in trust': they required the benefits of English law and firm government, of Christianity, educational and philanthropic provision generally, and of military protection from more ruthless exploiters. In return for such benefits, England had a right to expect loyalty, trade concessions and treaty rights. But the lesson of history was well understood—that the attempt to impose such conditions on emigrated Britons had lost us the American colonies, the most highly prized pearl of the first British Empire.

It required little imagination to see that the new 'white' colonies must be treated differently, and, in particular, given a substantial measure of control over their own affairs. The new policy was initiated in 1847, when Canada was granted a large degree of autonomy, her own parliament and a responsible minister, while Britain remained primarily responsible for foreign policy and defence. The process of self-government was thus begun which finally culminated in the Statute of Westminster of 1931.

The American colonies had been lost by England's attempt to control their trade and economic development. Now, Britain gradually abandoned her old colonial system by which the colonies had been obliged to trade only with the mother country. In 1825 Canada was permitted to trade with foreign countries, and in 1849 the repeal of the Navigation Acts brought free trade to all the colonies. By this time, the 'white empire' was firmly linked to Britain, not by political

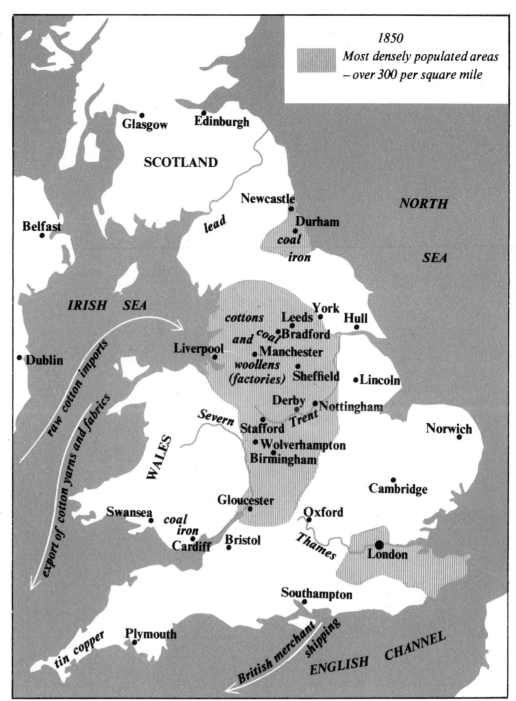

The Industrial Revolution was a period in English history (1750–1850), in which basic changes in the country's economic structure came about through a transition from an agricultural and commercial society to a modern industrialism.

bonds, but by common language and civilisation and by unquestioned loyalty to the Crown. Queen Victoria's adoption of the title 'Empress of India' was symbolic of the new role of the monarchy and of the strange power which a small island had to control the destinies of two hundred and forty million people throughout the world.

Britain's achievement

To other European countries in the first half of the nineteenth century Britain's success seemed remarkable and phenomenal. When thousands of foreign visitors attended the Great Exhibition in Hyde Park in 1851 they were impressed, even overwhelmed, by the industrial products and mechanical ingenuity of the British, as by the colonial pavilions displaying the resources of her far flung empire. Designed, in the Prince Consort's words, 'to illustrate the point of industrial development at which the whole of mankind has now arrived', it in fact demonstrated for all to see the immense wealth of Britain and the great lead which she enjoyed over all other nations.

Yet it is important to remember that this position had been only recently acquired, and, in the perspective of history, was comparatively short-lived. In 1800 France had been the 'great power' the conqueror of Europe, master of a vast empire, home of a philosophy that seemed destined to swamp the world. By 1870 Britain's position was

already coming to be challenged by newly industrialised nations, Germany and the United States, who seemed to possess in a marked degree the characteristics of industry and initiative of which Britain had thought herself the sole repository. Observers at the International Exhibition at Paris in 1867 were now struck, not so much by the British contribution, as by the remarkable progress of other countries.

Britain's tenure of unchallenged world leadership was, then, comparatively brief. She achieved it partly through the natural talents of her people and the abundant natural resources of her land, partly through the absence of any substantial rival. France after 1815 was defeated and exhausted, her economy virtually prostrate after a quarter of a century geared to war needs. Germany and Italy did not yet exist as nation-states until the processes of unification had been completed in 1870, while the United States of America, 'united' in name, were not so in any real sense as the Civil War of the 1860s was to demonstrate. None of these countries could yet command the political stability which seemed to be a necessary condition of rapid economic growth.

It would be a gross over-simplification to say that Britain in the nineteenth century chose to have an industrial rather than a political revolution. The evolution of democratic institutions went on alongside economic and social changes, often impelled by those very changes. On the continent political change frequently occurred which was not rooted in the economic fabric of society but was much more the product of philosophical ideas and intellectual ferment. Neither Robert Owen nor the Chartists ever brought Britain close to revolution, though Britain was the home of the first industrial proletariat and, in the Marxist logic, should have been the first to experience an open class war. The fact was that industrialisation enriched as many—perhaps more—than it impoverished, and in the course of time raised standards of living infinitely higher than they could ever have been under a rural economy. New wealth created new classes and new political parties which responded in a practical way to the pressures for change. In Europe such evolutionary change was often impossible, and there was no alternative to a sudden and violent overthrow of an existing regime. It is to this complicated story of political revolution that we now turn.

Above: the 80th Regiment defeating the Sikhs at the battle of Ferozeshah, 1845. In the second half of the century, violence gradually gave way to a more liberal policy towards the empire, of which Canada was the first country to benefit. (Bibliothèque Nationale, Paris.)

The springtime of nations

The rise of liberalism and nationalism in Europe; the revolutions of 1830 and 1848—
France leads the way; the Eastern Question; the fight for Greek independence;
the decline of Turkish power; the Crimean War.

The political history of Europe between 1815 and 1870 is largely the history of the undoing of the attempt by the victorious allies to reconstruct the old order throughout the lands once conquered by France. In this sense, the results of the French Revolution were enduring. In the face of strong liberal and nationalistic movements, it proved impossible to turn the clock back to repressive government, and the peoples of Europe—whether in Germany, Austria, Italy, Greece or in France itself—constantly erupted into open revolt against governments which denied them the principle of democratic participation. The real 'challenge of the nineteenth century' was, then, the challenge of revolution—the necessity of reconciling the legiti-

mate liberty of the individual with the ordered government of the state.

The peoples and the Holy Alliance

The peace treaties of 1815 had been designed not only to reorganise and make safe the frontiers of Europe, to punish France and reward her opponents, but also to conserve the firm position of tradition, order and religion against any possible return of revolution. It had been envisaged that there would be regular meetings of the four great powers—England, Prussia, Austria and Russia to maintain these principles against any attempt at disturbance. But from about

1820 onwards, what has been called 'the Metternich System' had to defend itself constantly against a mounting and double attack from liberalism and nationalism. These concepts were in theory distinct, though in practice frequently unified.

Liberalism was largely the heritage of the ideas spread by the French conquests (civil and political liberty and equality, the sovereignty of the people and the right to democratic government). It had the support of

Above: a view of Frankfurt in 1826 by Delkeskamp. The city was the seat of the diet of the German Confederation (1815–66). (Goethemuseum, Frankfurt.)

43

many of the middle classes who were hostile to rule by the minority and to the continuing powers and privileges of aristocracy, but they found ready allies for their cause among the growing body of industrial workers in the cities.

Nationalist feelings owed less to the French Revolution itself, more to the spirit of patriotism which the Napoleonic conquests had awoken in many peoples not previously remarkable for their national loyalty. It was also the case that the peace treaties of 1815 had divided populations with little consideration for such feelings so that, for example, the Rhineland was given to Prussia, and many Italians found themselves part of the Austrian dominions. Also, the policy of the allies of maintaining tiny principalities throughout Europe — inspired partly by a fear of powerful states — took no account of this growing sense of nationhood and desire for unity among peoples who shared a common language and culture.

Top: the assassination of Kotzebue, 23 March 1819, at Mannheim, by a student of theology, Karl Ludwig Sand. Kotzebue had been a spy for the tsar and had published a weekly paper in Weimar attacking all those who strove for liberty and independence.
Above: the execution of Sand.
(Historisches Museum, Frankfurt.)

Right: Louis I of Bavaria in his coronation robes. At first a liberal, he later became reactionary, and this together with his scandalous affair with the dancer Lola Montez, forced him to abdicate in 1848. (Alte Pinakothek, Munich.)
Far right: the wounded soldiers of the Grand Imperial Army returning to France. The French occupation of Italy and Spain had sown the seeds of liberal and republican sympathies in those countries. (Bibliothèque Nationale, Paris.)

Germany: the Congresses of Carlsbad and Vienna

The first congress planned by the allies was held at Aix-la-Chapelle in 1818, and was concerned exclusively with French affairs. It was decided that occupation troops could now be evacuated, and that France under the re-established Bourbon monarchy of Louis XVIII was sufficiently stable to join the Quadruple Alliance. But in Germany revolutionary agitation had already begun, led by a student body, the *Burschenschaft*, who in the course of a demonstration had burnt reactionary literature and other symbols of militarism. The rulers of three German states—Bavaria, Baden and Wurtemburg—were sufficiently alarmed to grant democratic constitutions to their peoples. Shortly afterwards, the assassination by a student of the journalist Kotzebue, a Russian agent who had been leading a campaign against liberal and nationalistic ideas, de-

termined Metternich, the chancellor of Austria, to act. At Vienna in 1820 the German princes outlawed the *Burschenschaft*, imposed press censorship and brought the universities under strict control, though Metternich was unable to persuade the South German rulers to withdraw the recently granted constitutions.

Revolutions in Cadiz and Naples

In Spain, the restoration of the despotic King Ferdinand VII had brought to power a party which represented the deepest reaction. The country was now plunged into one of the unhappiest episodes in her unhappy history.

During Spain's struggle for independence against the French it had been shown that the local parliaments or *cortes*, where liberals were usually dominant, could produce enlightened and effective policies, but after the

restoration of Ferdinand the *cortes* were ignored, thousands of liberal patriots were branded as French sympathisers, a strict censorship was imposed and despotic rule and corruption triumphed everywhere. The only resort left to liberals was to form secret societies against the government and to engage in plots which always failed.

In 1820 in Cadiz, however, a much more serious situation arose. An army of 20,000 men had been assembled to be sent to South America to suppress revolution in the Spanish colonies there. Colonel Riego led many of the troops in revolt, demanding a liberal constitution. Successful in Andalusia, insurrection spread quickly to the provinces of Galicia and Catalonia, and the king was forced to adopt the constitution and to dismiss his unpopular ministers.

The apparent victory of the Spanish liberals now spread revolutionary ideas across the Mediterranean to Italy. Italy in 1815 was, in Metternich's famous phrase, merely 'a

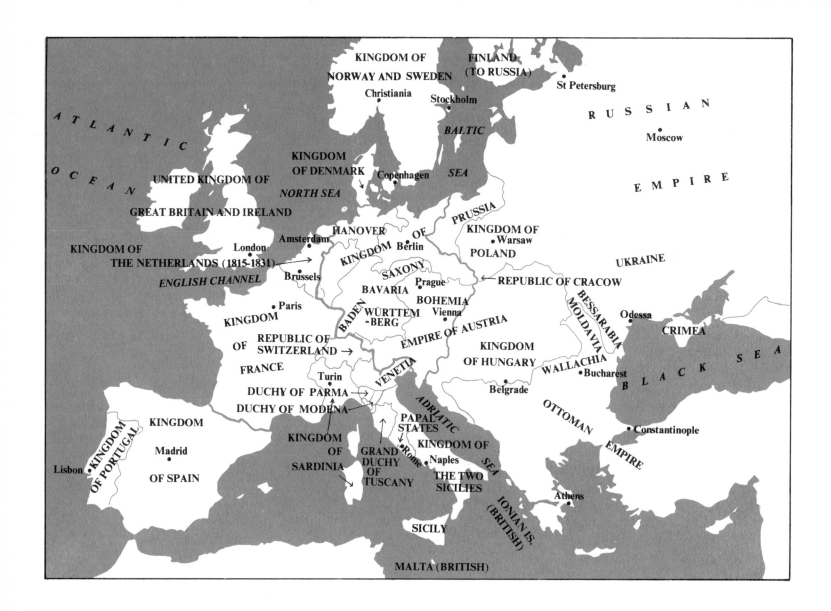

KINGDOM OF
NORWAY AND SWEDEN

FINLAND
(TO RUSSIA)

Christiania • • Stockholm

• St Petersburg

BALTIC

R U S S I A N

ATLANTIC

• Moscow

OCEAN

E M P I R E

SEA

KINGDOM
OF DENMARK

• Copenhagen

UNITED KINGDOM OF

NORTH SEA

GREAT BRITAIN AND IRELAND

PRUSSIA

HANOVER

KINGDOM OF

KINGDOM
OF DENMARK

KINGDOM OF
• Warsaw

Amsterdam •

KINGDOM OF

POLAND

London •

• Berlin

KINGDOM OF

UKRAINE

THE NETHERLANDS (1815-1831)

SAXONY

ENGLISH CHANNEL

Brussels •

REPUBLIC OF CRACOW

BAVARIA

BESSARABIA

• Paris

BOHEMIA

• Prague

MOLDAVIA

• Odessa

KINGDOM

WÜRTTEM
-BERG

• Vienna

CRIMEA

BADEN

OF

REPUBLIC OF
SWITZERLAND →

EMPIRE OF AUSTRIA

KINGDOM
OF HUNGARY

WALLACHIA

B L A C K   S E A

FRANCE

VENETIA

• Bucharest

Turin •

DUCHY OF PARMA →

• Belgrade

DUCHY OF MODENA →

ADRIATIC

OTTOMAN

PAPAL
STATES

• Constantinople

KINGDOM

• Rome

KINGDOM OF

KINGDOM
OF
SARDINIA

GRAND
DUCHY
OF
TUSCANY

• Naples

THE TWO
SICILIES

SEA

EMPIRE

KINGDOM OF PORTUGAL

KINGDOM

• Madrid

KINGDOM OF PORTUGAL

OF SPAIN

IONIAN IS.
(BRITISH)

• Athens

Lisbon •

SICILY

MALTA (BRITISH)

Above: Europe after the Congress of Vienna. The congress was called to arrange a settlement of European affairs after the defeat of Napoleon Bonaparte. Among territorial changes were the establishment of the German Confederation, the union of a Polish kingdom with Russia, the union of Norway and Sweden, and the unification of the United Provinces and the Austrian Netherlands (Belgium) as the Netherlands.

After the Congress of Vienna the great powers attempted to reimpose the ancien régime on Europe, restoring dispossessed rulers, reviving pomp and pageantry and suppressing liberal movements.
Left: a parade in Berlin (1822) painted by Krüger and (right) a detail from the same painting. (Nationalgalerie, East Berlin.)

Below: the emperor Frederick of Austria is crowned in 1835. A sick man, he abdicated in 1848. During his monarchy confusion and disorder reigned in the administration of the Austrian Empire. (Royal Palace, Prague.)

Bottom: Prince Augustus of Prussia, who devoted himself to perfecting the artillery of the Prussian army. He is standing in front of a portrait of Madam Récamier, whose salon was famous throughout Europe as the meeting place of political and literary figures. (Charlottenburg Castle, West Berlin.)

geographical expression'. She was a collection of independent states—Piedmont-Sardinia in the north, Parma, Modena, Tuscany and the Papal States in the centre and the Kingdom of the Two Sicilies in the south. Austria possessed the kingdom of Lombardy-Venetia and wielded great influence in the affairs of many of the states. Everywhere there was censorship and police suppression of any attempt at liberal agitation. As in Spain, middle-class liberals had formed secret societies, known locally as the *Carboneria*, because their members met in the woods like charcoal burners.

Yet, at the news of the Spanish insurrection, army officers in Naples called out their troops in revolt in July 1820, and their leader, General Pepe, forced Ferdinand I of Naples to accept a democratic constitution similar to that granted in Spain. To many it seemed that this pattern of events marked the beginning of the end of autocracy.

Troppau and Laibach: reaction in Italy

Metternich's fear was that revolution would now spread through the whole of Italy. In 1820 the emperors of Austria and Russia, the King of Prussia and French and English representatives met together at the Congress of Troppau in Silesia. Metternich converted the tsar to the idea of armed intervention against liberal movements, despite opposition from Castlereagh (the English foreign secretary) and the French delegate, who saw it as a move to increase Austrian influence in Italy.

At the Congress of Laibach, in January 1821, armed intervention was agreed on. Austrian troops dispersed the forces of General Pepe and entered Naples: the constitution was abolished and liberal leaders executed. But meanwhile, revolutionary ferment had spread to students and army officers in Lombardy, with the object of freeing their state from Austrian domination. The king, Victor Emmanuel I, who had been

restored by the allied powers in 1814, was hated by the liberals because of his reactionary policies, and now abdicated in favour of his brother Charles Felix (1821). He lost little time in calling in the Austrians, who easily defeated the liberal forces at Novara.

The tide was also turning towards reaction in Spain. The liberal reformers who had secured the constitution from Ferdinand VII had no experience of government, and did not succeed in maintaining order or in putting reforms into practice. Plots and risings occurred ceaselessly, giving Ferdinand the opportunity to call in outside help. The so-called 'Holy Alliance' of Russia, Austria, Prussia and France, formed in theory to conduct the affairs of Europe in accordance with Christian principles, but in fact as an instrument for maintaining the status quo, was more than willing to respond. The Congress of Verona (September 1822) was thus called to deal with the Spanish question.

The congress of Verona: repression in Spain

Canning, who had succeeded Castlereagh as the British foreign secretary, declared himself strongly opposed to intervention in the internal affairs of Spain or her rebellious South American colonies. In officially recognising their independence Britain was, he announced, 'calling in the New World to redress the balance of the Old'. His message was lost on the other European powers. France was especially anxious to suppress revolution so close to her borders, as well as to demonstrate the military might of the restored Bourbon monarchy. Approval was given by the congress (Britain having withdrawn) to her intervention, and in April 1823 a French army of 100,000 entered Spain and quickly defeated the rebels at Cadiz and elsewhere. The repression which followed throughout the next ten years was more ferocious even than that in Italy, the liberal leader Riego and his comrades being mercilessly hunted down, shot and massa-

cred. Until 1828 French troops continued to garrison fortresses throughout Spain in order to buttress the repressive policies of the Spanish minister of justice, Francisco de Calomarde.

The revolution of 1830 and the rise of Mazzini

For a few years in the 1820s the forces of reaction in Europe seemed triumphant: Italy and Spain lay prostrate under the heel of foreign autocratic domination. But in 1830 the Paris Revolution and the replacement on the French throne of the Bourbons by the 'bourgeois king' Louis Philippe, caused reverberations throughout Europe which seemed to echo the storming of the Bastille by the Paris mob forty years earlier. Exiled *Carboneria* in Paris not unnaturally looked for French assistance in a new attempt to rid Italy of the hated Austrians. Secret revolutionary societies were again active in Lombardy, the Papal States and throughout central Italy.

Revolution in fact broke out in Modena in February 1831, quickly spreading to Parma, Bologna and the Romagna. In March an unlawful assembly at Bologna proclaimed the union and independence of the rebel provinces. Again, however, Metternich was master of the situation. He persuaded Louis Philippe that two of the Bonaparte princes were in the movement, and that it therefore constituted a danger to the security of France. Austrian armies suppressed the rebels in Parma and Modena. In Bologna the rebels were either dispersed or arrested. Louis Philippe himself sent an expeditionary force to occupy Ancona.

By now the *Carboneria* had been thoroughly discredited by their repeated failures and apparent inability to organise effectively. The spirit of revolt in Italy was kept alive, however, by writers and propagandists, many of them in exile. By far the most influential was a young Genoese, Guiseppe Mazzini, who founded a movement in Paris in 1832 known as 'Young Italy'. Its aim was a democratic republic, free of foreign domination: its slogan 'Unity and Republic, God and People, Thought and Action'. Mazzini's romantic personality attracted many followers, but his vague idealism was hardly what the situation demanded. More realistic policies were advocated by the Abbé Gioberti, who proposed a federation of the Italian states under the papacy; by the historian Balbo, who gave to Piedmont the role of unifying Italy, and by Count Cavour premier of Sardinia, who foresaw the necessity of defeating Austria militarily before independence could be achieved. All these ideas and aspirations were eventually to fuse in the *Risorgimento*.

Germany and Poland

In 1815 Germany, like Italy, was a mere 'geographical expression'. It consisted of thirty-nine independent states, some powerful like Prussia and Bavaria, others no more than tiny principalities, though equally proud of their separate identities. As yet there was little thought of national unity, though, as elsewhere in Europe, democratic thought had gained ground during the Napoleonic period.

The events of 1830 led to renewed demands for liberal reform in several states, and the rulers of Saxony, Bavaria, Brunswick and Hesse-Cassel were made sufficiently uneasy to grant constitutions to their peoples. The *Burschenschaft* was also re-formed in universities throughout Germany. As always, Metternich was alarmed at these stirrings of independent thought, and, supported by Prussia, was able to get rigorous measures adopted by the Diet of Frankfurt (July 1832) including press censorship and the banning of unauthorised clubs and meetings. The writings of Heinrich Heine, Georg Büchner and others were banned as subversive, and pressure was put on France to

expel the large number of political refugees who had gathered there.

In fact, the idea of German unity was making progress in quite a different way. Prussia took the first step by founding the *Zollverein* or customs union, allowing the free passage of goods between states instead of the heavy tolls formerly charged. As a free trade measure it was a spectacular success, greatly increasing the level of commerce and economic activity generally: one state after another joined, until by 1834 nearly all had done so. More than this, however, the *Zollverein* facilitated the movement of people and ideas in Germany, undermined local prejudices and demonstrated the growing leadership of Prussia in German affairs.

Liberalism had an even harder struggle in Poland. This unhappy country had often been the subject of dispute and division among the powers, most recently in 1815 when the Duchy of Warsaw was created into a separate state and made part of the dominions of Russia. In theory it was endowed with its own parliament voting laws and taxes, as well as its own army, though this was under the command of the Tsar Alexander's own brother, the brutal and authoritarian Grand Duke Constantine. The tsar's promise of a

liberal, constitutional regime showed no sign of fulfilment.

In the other parts of Poland—Galatia which had been ceded to Austria and Posnan which had been given to Prussia—there existed assemblies which were only partially representative of the people. Polish patriots, many officers and intellectuals, had long been meeting together in secret societies, awaiting the moment to rise in support of unification and independence. At the news of the revolution in France in 1830, Constantine foolishly ordered the mobilisation of the Polish army, and rumour quickly had it that he intended to use Polish troops to suppress the French liberals. The Poles in Warsaw rebelled, the Diet proclaiming the independence of the country and the deposition of the tsar (January 1831).

In spite of sympathy from France, none of the powers intervened to help the Poles, and the rebellion was soon crushed by the Russian army. There followed a more than usually severe repression, with mass hangings and deportations. Universities were closed, lands were confiscated and Russian made the official language of the country. Thousands of Polish émigrés fled to France where they continued to hold up the torch of freedom.

Faced with Austrian domination, the movement for Italian independence had little success in the early years.
Above: a parade of Austrian troops, 1833. A painting by Angelo Inganni. (Heeresgeschichtliches Museum, Vienna.)
Ironically it was in Vienna itself in 1848 that the most dangerous revolution occurred for the future of the empire.
Above right: the barricades at the Tosa Gate, Milan, on 22 March 1848. Anonymous painting. (Museo del Risorgimento, Milan.)
Below right: Marshal Radetzky after the Austrians' victory over the Sardinians at the battle of Novara, 1849. Painting by Albrecht Adam. (Heeresgeschichtliches Museum, Vienna.)

51

The birth of modern Belgium

Only one of the many revolutions of 1830 was, in fact, successful—that of Belguim. In 1815 this little state had been given to the Netherlands—before that she had been, in turn, ruled by Spain, Austria, and France. Although the union of industrial Belgium with agricultural Holland had been an economic success, there was almost nothing in common between the two countries. Belgians spoke French (or Flemish), not Dutch; they were Catholics, not Protestants; they were in outlook liberal, not authoritarian. Moreover, the constitution was heavily weighted against them, with the Dutch William of Orange as king, only one Belgian minister out of a cabinet of seven, and less than 300 officers out of an army of 2,000.

In 1830 an alliance of Catholics and liberals rose in revolution, set up a provisional government and proclaimed the independence of Belgium. Everything now depended on the attitude of the great powers, and particularly that of Britain whose traditional policy it was that the Low Countries should not be under the control of a strong, and possibly hostile, country. For this reason Britain opposed the offer of the Belgian crown to the Duke of Nemours, son of Louis Philippe of France. At the conference of London (December 1830) the powers formally recognised the independence and—significantly for the future—the neutrality of Belgium. The crown was accepted by a German prince, Leopold of Saxe-Coburg-Gotha, who became King Leopold I. Holland, who had still not accepted the situation, attacked the new country the next year, but England and France quickly came to her aid and forced the Dutch to withdraw. Holland officially recognised the existence of Belgium in 1839.

The crisis of 1848

The historian De Tocqueville wrote in 1848, 'Here begins again the French Revolution—this is exactly the same'. In fact, the events of 1848-9, though more widespread, violent and spectacular, were much more akin to those of 1821 or 1830 than to the localised events of 1789. As before, there was the same mixture of liberal and nationalist aspirations, but a third element was now significant for the first time in the social conflict bred by industrialisation. By 1848 many European cities had sizeable working classes which had been almost non-existent at the time of the French Revolution—populations of factory workers condemned to be the slaves of machines, confined to miserable lives in tenements and slums, who were beginning to demand a voice in their own destiny. Significantly, in Paris in 1848 the workers actually rose against the liberal middle classes, so opening a new chapter in the history of revolution which was to end in

52

It was in March 1848 that revolution broke out in Vienna. Metternich was forced to flee from the capital in a laundry van. In the street fighting the people had the upper hand. Many of the middle classes joined the National Guard to maintain the principles of the revolution.

Left: the National Guard in Anhof Square, Vienna. Anonymous painting. (Heeresgeschichtliches Museum, Vienna.)

Revolutions also occurred in several German cities.

Right: the deputy Kossler asks for an armistice by waving the white flag.

Below: in Berlin and Frankfurt bitter fighting continued until Frederick William IV ordered the cease-fire. (Historisches Museum, Frankfurt.)

Der Barricadenkampf in Berlin.

the accession to power of Napoleon III, the nephew of the former emperor. In the events of the mid-century, social and economic issues were fundamentally more important than the purely political.

More immediately, the events of 1848 had their origin in the Irish potato disease of 1845-6. This spread to the continent, causing an acute shortage of wheat which doubled prices in 1846–7 and resulted in food riots in France, Germany, Belgium and Italy. Commercial crises developed, as the banks used up stocks of gold to pay for wheat and could advance no more credit: there were numerous bankruptcies and a general lack of commercial confidence which resulted in heavy unemployment. While prices rose eighty to a hundred per cent wages were cut by an average of twenty per cent.

The events of 1848 are confused and complicated, Political demands are inextricably mingled with the social discontent, and there is an interaction or chain process which seems to sweep the infection across Europe, invading first one country, then the next. Revolution occurred first in Italy in January 1848, then in France in February, next in Vienna in March. By June the tide was running at its height, by the end of the summer it was already on the ebb.

The revolution in Italy

In Italy the immediate cause of revolution was a combination of the economic crisis and the election of a liberal pope, Pius IX, from whom a lead in liberal reforms was expected. By the end of 1847 the whole peninsular was in ferment, and independent risings shortly broke out in widely separated states—in Sicily, demanding her independence from the Kingdom of Naples, and in Lombardy in the north, where a boycott of Austrian tobacco sparked off bitter street

fighting in Milan. Rulers were sufficiently alarmed to give way to demands for democratic constitutions in Naples, Tuscany and in Piedmont, where Charles Albert invited the revolutionary, Balbo, to join the government. In the Papal States Pius IX accepted laymen as cabinet ministers, and he too proposed a new constitution.

The most serious fighting was in Milan, where the revolution took the form of a truly national struggle against the Austrians. After five days of bitter street warfare (18–22 March) Austrian troops were forced to evacuate Milan, while in Venice, the other Austrian possession in northern Italy, the garrison was forced to capitulate by the patriots, led by Daniele Manin and Niccolo Tommaseo. The dukes of Parma and Modena, puppets of Austria, were also replaced by provisional governments.

With independent revolutions occurring throughout the peninsula, it seemed that the time had come for some state to take the leadership in the movement for unity and independence. The state of Piedmont in the north west, was ruled by Charles Albert and he and Count Cavour, who was then his chief minister, believed that it was Piedmont's destiny, to lead an Italian crusade which would rid the country of the foreigner and unite the states under the Piedmontese dynasty. Piedmont entered the war on 24 March without any alliance from an outside prince or, indeed, the other provisional governments of Italy. For a time it seemed that Charles Albert's calculation was justified. Volunteers flocked in from Rome, Tuscany, and Naples, and Manin collaborated by organising the defence of Venice.

At first there were early successes against the Austrians at Goito and Peschiera. Soon, however, the alliance began to falter. There were suspicions that Piedmont had territorial ambitions on other states, and that her part in the movement was not entirely

After the crushing of the revolution in Vienna, the king of Prussia took up the struggle against the National Assembly. In December Berlin was attacked again by troops.
Left: a barricade in the streets of Berlin. (Kunstbibliothek, West Berlin.)
Above: the revolution took toll of over 200 victims in Frankfurt. (Historisches Museum, Frankfurt.)
Prague was the first capital to be affected by the revolutionary movement. Palacký, president of the Pan-Slav Congress, declared: 'I am not German, I am Czech, Slav by origin, and the little that I have is all at the service of my nation'.
Right: the barricades in Prague, 1848. (Museum of Czech Literature, Prague.)

unselfish: Pius IX decided to withdraw the papal forces on the ground that the pope could not engage in war against Austria, the protector of the Catholic faith. Two more members of the alliance, Naples and Tuscany, quickly followed suit. Piedmont and Venice now remained alone against the might of Austria.

The revolution in Austria

In Austria-Hungary, the ancient empire of the Habsburgs, the problems were complex. In the capital, Vienna, the revolution was primarily one of students and middle-class liberals in opposition to the absolutist régime of Metternich, the chancellor. Elsewhere nationalism was the main impulse, and democracy only a secondary issue. The empire in fact covered a vast territory, inhabited by peoples of widely different beliefs, language and culture, and the motives of their protest were often tangled and obscure.

While Austria herself was largely German in language and customs, Hungary was mainly Slav. In theory a separate kingdom, she shared the common rule of the Habs-

burgs and was in most respects subservient to Austria. For many years there had been a movement for national independence in Hungary, led by some of the great landowners in what was still primarily a peasant country. There was also a body of liberal rebels led by men like Louis Kossuth and Ferenc Deák, working for democratic reform and the development of a modern economic system. The fact that even Kossuth was less liberal in his attitude towards the Roumanian and Croat minorities within Hungary was something that Metternich was subsequently able to exploit.

Bohemia was also a centre of national feeling in the empire—though she had not existed as an independent state since the seventeenth century, and had since undergone a long process of Germanisation. The Czechs had experienced a national re-awakening led by poets and historians like Jan Kollár and František Palacký, and already by 1845 the Diet of Prague was showing opposition to the rule of Vienna.

In many parts of the empire therefore, nationalists were waiting for the signal to rise. The day after the Paris revolution, on 12 February 1848, the students of Vienna

began attacking the government forces, and after a few days of bitter fighting Metternich was forced to flee to safety hidden in a laundry van.

The emperor Ferdinand granted freedom of the press and of assembly, and promised a constitution. When published, it was thought insufficiently liberal, and a general insurrection then took place in May, at which Ferdinand now agreed to government by a constitutional assembly elected by universal suffrage. Vienna was firmly under the control of the students and the National Guard, formed by the middle classes to defend the revolution.

Elsewhere in the empire the revolution also seemed to be successful. In Hungary, led by Kossuth, independence was gradually being won, as the country gained the right to have its own army and financial system. In Prague a provisional government had been formed under the historian Palacký and a pan-Slav congress had met with a view to uniting the scattered Slavs of the empire into one state.

In Germany, too, there had been outbreaks of students, workers and peasants from February onwards, in the Rhineland

in the north as well as in several southern states. Some rulers granted free speech and the right of constitutional assembly, abolished feudalism and the status of serfdom. The old King Louis of Bavaria abdicated in favour of his son Maximilian, while in Berlin a bloody riot in March forced King Frederick William IV of Prussia to withdraw his forces and promise a universally elected government. Tendencies towards national unity were also becoming noticeable. At Frankfurt an assembly of 600 delegates drawn from all parts of Germany agreed on the election of a constitutional parliament to prepare the way for a new, unified government for the whole country. This hopeful experiment in fact never had much likelihood of success. The parliament consisted mainly of notables and intellectuals, the commercial and business interests holding aloof. It soon showed itself to be a powerless debating chamber, quite impotent as an instrument of government.

Nevertheless, the very extent of the revolutions throughout Germany, Austria and Italy served to indicate the imminent break-up of the old Habsburg Empire. That it was able to survive the crisis was in no way due

to the monarchy, but to the loyalty of the professional army in the face of disaster.

Failure in Italy: the march of Radetzky

In spite of the Viennese rising, Field Marshal Radetzky, the Austrian commander, decided to send his army first against the Italians. The Piedmontese army was attacked and defeated at Custozza (July 1848), Milan was occupied and Piedmont forced to accept an armistice. Already, two of the objectives of the Risorgimento had failed—to unify the Italian states under the head of the House of Savoy (Piedmont) and to involve the papacy in the national struggle. But there still remained Mazzini's ideal of a republic which would sweep away all incompetent monarchies.

Mazzinians were strongest in Rome itself, where many refugees had fled from other states, and in November 1848 Count Rossi, Pius IX's anti-democratic minister, was stabbed. The Pope left the city in the hands of Mazzinians, who established a republic there in February 1849. Both Florence and Venice, under Daniele Manin, also pro-

claimed republican constitutions. New hope dawned of an Italy freed from both foreign oppressors and tyrannical rulers. Mazzini himself was triumphantly welcomed in Rome in March, and his lieutenant, Giuseppe Garibaldi, organised the army there.

This growth of republican feeling alarmed Charles Albert of Piedmont, who saw his chances of leading the Italian movement slipping away. Breaking the armistice, he re-entered the war, but was utterly defeated by the Austrians at Novara (23 March 1849) and abdicated in favour of his son, Victor Emmanuel. Austria followed up her success by invading the smaller states of Parma, Modena and Tuscany, and restoring the dukes there. At the same time, Ferdinand of Naples regained control of Sicily.

In Rome, the success of the republicans now began to alarm foreign powers and, in particular, France. The Catholic party there wished to support the Pope, while national interests were in favour of a military success which would limit the power of Austria in the peninsular. An expeditionary force of 7,000 men which arrived at Civitavecchia was beaten back by Garibaldi's amateur army, but with the help of rein-

The defeat of the German revolution.
Above: defeated, the middle classes were
forced to surrender their arms to the troops.
Right: the burial of the victims of the
barricades was the occasion for an imposing
funeral procession on 22 March 1848.
Subsequent repression was to frustrate any
progress towards liberal reform. (Zeughaus,
East Berlin.)

forcements, the French army entered Rome in July 1849, and Mazzini was forced to flee. Resistance continued only in Venice, but worn down by famine and disease she, too, capitulated in August. The heroism and sacrifice of the Italian patriots had seemed to be in vain. Only in one state—Piedmont—did there remain a ray of hope. Though militarily defeated the new king, Victor Emmanuel, refused to abandon his constitutional regime. Advised by his minister, Cavour, he reflected on the lessons of 1848–9 and planned for the future.

The defeat of the Austrian revolution

What Radetzky had done in Italy, Marshal Windischgraetz was to do in Austria. He was a man of the sternest principle, once having declared that 'Blood is the only remedy for all the ills of the century—communism, radicalism, impiety and atheism'. Prague was bombarded, besieged and forced to submit to a military dictatorship in June 1848. The imperial cause was helped by the disunity of the rebel states, and particularly by the enmity between the Croats and the Hungarians. Hungary, under Louis Kossuth, had now come to the point of open rebellion against Austria, and the emperor cunningly gave command of the opposing army to the Croat 'Governor' Jellachich. At the news of the war against Hungary, the Viennese liberals again rose in revolt, hanged the Minister of War and forced Ferdinand to flee the capital.

In October Windischgraetz laid siege to Vienna, while the Croat army prevented aid coming from Hungary. Eventually the city fell and the democratic leaders were shot and their supporters arrested in great numbers. The emperor, now somewhat discredited by his weak handling of the situation, was, however, persuaded to abdicate in favour of his nephew, the Archduke Francis Joseph (December 1848).

The agony of Hungary

From September 1848 Kossuth had headed the revolutionary government of Hungary and led the army of resistance against Austria. There was, however, an obvious limit to the capability of largely untrained volunteers against what was probably the best army in Europe, and despite all their efforts the Hungarians could not prevent Austrian and Croatian troops from entering the country in February 1849. By the spring, however, Kossuth had almost miraculously recovered the situation, having driven the enemy forces from the country, and so proclaimed the independence of Hungary and deposition of the hated Habsburgs (April 1849).

The emperor now entered into negotiations with the tsar, Nicholas I, for assistance. Nicholas was only too ready to

After the failure of the Parliament of Frankfurt, a hundred republican deputies decided to meet at Stuttgart. They were dispersed by troops from Württemberg (18 September 1848).
Left: the republicans tear up paving stones for weapons. (Historisches Museum, Frankfurt.)

help Austria in return for a free hand in the East against Turkey, and immediately put an army of 130,000 men at the disposal of his ally. This meant virtual annihilation for the rebels. Kossuth resigned and sought refuge in Turkey. The last Hungarians capitulated at Vilagos in August 1849, and bitter reprisals followed against the patriots and all who had aided them. For the time being Francis Joseph had patched up his tottering empire: he was to live long enough to witness its final collapse in 1916.

Defeat in Germany

At Frankfurt, the constituent parliament from all parts of Germany continued to debate the formation of a unified empire in place of the thirty-nine independent states. After endlesss discussions the hereditary crown of the new empire was offered to King Frederick William IV of Prussia, in spite of the protests of Austria and of the south German states who disliked the idea of a Protestant sovereign. There was, in fact, little choice in the matter. Prussia was incomparably the strongest of the German states, had re-established firm government in her own country and had demonstrated her ability to lead through the idea of the *Zollverein*. The only possible contender was Bavaria, who had considerable influence over the Catholic states but was less powerful economically and militarily. But although Frederick William would have dearly liked an imperial crown, he was unwilling to accept one 'from the public streets, like that of Louis Philippe, a crown of rubbish made of clay and mud'. His chief minister, Bismarck, a firm believer in the divine right of kings, supported his decision.

Frederick William's rejection proved to be the death-blow for the Frankfurt Parliament. The Prussian deputies withdrew, and there was now no hope of effective leadership. But in numerous other German states—the Palatinate, Baden-Baden and Saxony—there were risings in the summer of 1849 and, significantly, these were much more working-class movements for social and economic reform than middle-class demands for nationalism or liberalism. The young Karl Marx, who was publishing the *Rhine Gazette* in Cologne at this time, learned much about the dynamics of the class struggle form a situation in which the middle classes were increasingly allied with the nobility in fear of proletarian revolution.

But although Frederick William had refused the offer of an imperial crown from the people, he had not renounced the ambition of German leadership on his own terms. He now negotiated with the kings of Saxony and Hanover a scheme for unity to which twenty-eight of the German states were ready to agree: a congress at Erfurt was planned to settle the final arrangements. He had, however, to face the jealousy and distrust of outside powers. Austria, who

The Eastern Question.
Above: Ali Pasha of Janina in 1788. After extending his authority over Albania, he exterminated the Christian population who had resisted Turkish domination. By 1814, as a result of cunning diplomacy, he was master of Albania, Epirus and part of Thessaly, but he had now become too dangerous to the sultan: his army was besieged in Janina and Ali killed.
Left: the pasha's army at Tricala. (Bibliothèque Nationale, Paris.)
Above right: Colonel Fabvier, one of the many Frenchmen to give their services in the cause of Greek independence.
Right: a Greek soldier. (Bibliothèque Nationale, Paris.)

Above: Constantin Canaris, born at Ipsara in 1790, *one of the heroes of Greek independence. A sailor by profession, he later held office as a cabinet minister. (Bibliothèque Nationale, Paris.)*

had now crushed her Hungarian revolt, strongly opposed this growth in the power of Prussia, as did the tsar. Saxony and Hanover were persuaded to withdraw from negotiations, and Prussia continued her plan only with the northern states.

Austria had decided that Prussia must be humiliated, and that her own leadership of German affairs should be unchallenged. Schwarzenberg, the new chancellor of Austria who had succeeded Metternich, devoutly believed that there could be no Reich (German commonwealth) without Austria, and sought an occasion to break up the league of princes which Prussia was sponsoring. The opportunity arose over Hesse-Cassel, where the tyrannical duke had recently been deposed: Prussia supported his subjects, Austria demanded his restoration. For a while the rival armies of Prussia and Austria faced each other poised for war, but two days later at Olmutz Prussia gave way, and accepted all the Austrian demands including the dissolution of the proposed union.

By 1850 there seemed little left of 'the year of revolutions'. Austria had apparently re-established firm government in her empire and prestige among the German states. Democratic and nationalist movements had equally failed to take root, and the sufferings of the peoples of Europe seemed to be in vain. The enduring results were a liberal constitution in Piedmont, and the abolition of feudalism in Austria and Germany. Moreover, two men had emerged from the crisis who were to become central figures on the

European stage during the next twenty years, Cavour in Piedmont and Bismarck in Prussia. Under their leadership, the course of German and Italian unity was to take a new and decisive turn. But for the immediate future, the attention of Europe was drawn to the East, where similar nationalist aspirations were beginning to open great cracks in the once powerful Turkish Empire.

The Eastern Question

At the beginning of the nineteenth century the Turkish Empire, despite an already long history of decadence, still remained a vast conglomeration of states placed at the crossroads of three continents, Europe, Africa and Asia. Her territories covered the great peninsular of the Balkans, extended eastwards into Asia Minor and westwards along the North African coast as far as Algeria. Yet it was not so much the strength as the weakness of the Turkish Empire that produced the Eastern Question of the nineteenth century. Her declining power and supposed imminent collapse roused the territorial ambitions of both Russia and Austria. Britain was also concerned since she had no wish to see a strong power in this area which might endanger her trading routes to India and the Far East.

But the European powers were also interested in the affairs of the Orient on grounds of religion. The Turkish Empire, officially Muslim in faith, contained substantial minorities of Christians within its

Above: Mehemet Ali, pasha of Egypt and founder of the Egyptian royal house.
Right: the battle of Navarino in 1827. Shortly after the British, French and Russian fleets arrived at the roads of Navarino, some shots were accidently fired at the flagship of the French admiral. Within a few hours the Egyptian fleet had been sent to the bottom.
Far right: an Albanian Christian.
(Bibliothèque Nationale, Paris.)

borders who were regarded as *raia* (no more than cattle). They were subject to many special disabilities, taxes and dues which made the despised *raia* very much the most profitable subjects of the empire. Only if converted to Islam could they become full citizens, but the Turks, who wanted to keep the Christians weak and vulnerable, did not encourage such additions to Allah. In general, the Christians maintained their beliefs as members of the Greek Orthodox Church, of which Russia regarded herself as the protector.

For many years groups of rebels—half-patriots, half-brigands—had sought independence of the Turkish yoke. Here, too, the French Revolution had spread ideas of democracy and independence, and in the disturbed conditions of war bands of Serbian *haidouks* and Greek *palikares*, forerunners

of modern freedom-fighters, had begun to attack the hated Turkish army. Ever since 1804 the Serbs had been rebelling under their leader Kara George, and had suffered terrible reprisals. In 1815 revolution broke out again led by Miloš Obrenovich, but this time the Sultan acted with more prudence, fearing the possibility of intervention on the part of Russia on the side of the Serbs. Obrenovich was granted the title 'Chief of the Serbs' and made a pasha, responsible for the government of the province. The Turkish Empire had unwittingly taken the first step towards its own dissolution.

The awakening of Greece

'Come, children of the Hellenes, the hour of glory has arrived. . . . Macedonians, rise up like wild beasts: spill the blood of all

tyrants . . .' This song, based on the 'Marseillaise', appeared in 1797 at the beginning of the movement for Greek independence. In fact, the Greeks were among the most favoured subjects of the Ottoman Empire, allowed to practise their religion under their own Patriarch, holding four of the great offices of state, and largely monopolising the trade of the shore of the Mediterranean with their great merchant fleet. It was this measure of freedom and power that gave the Greeks their desire for more, that magnified their sense of injustice and reminded them of their former glories.

Significantly, the movement for independence sprang from the wealthy merchant communities spread around the Mediterranean shores and islands, traders who could command between them 600 ships manned by 17,000 sailors. In the great

Turkish city of Constantinople Greeks dominated the *Phanar* (the business quarter) and furnished numerous of the Sultan's administrators. In Odessa on the Black Sea Greeks had formed a secret society, the *Hetairie*, to prepare for revolution. Throughout the ports and the islands a secret network was gradually built up, linking the Greek communities together in a dream of freedom.

In 1821 Alexander Ypsilanti, a general of Greek origin who was in Russian service, was appointed military leader of the movement. The time seemed propitious, as the Sultan was occupied with a revolt of the Pasha of Janina, who was trying to establish his own dynasty in Albania. Ypsilanti now called on the Greeks to rise (March 1821) and the archbishop of Patras launched an appeal for independence. The campaign was, in fact, ill-led, and failed to receive

Scenes from the Crimean War.
Above: the Light Brigade at the battle of
Inkerman. Earlier, through a disputed
error in orders, the Earl of Cardigan had
led 670 light cavalry in a hopeless charge
against the Russian guns at Balaklava,
killing or wounding two-thirds of his men.
Left: Balaklava, looking out to sea, 1854.
(Bibliothèque Nationale, Paris.)

the expected outside support from Russia; the rising in Wallachia was easily crushed by the formidable Turkish janissaries (soldiers, originally forming the Sultans's guard). But at sea, on the islands and in the Morea, bitter guerrilla fighting continued which the Turks could not suppress.

The savage war

By the beginning of 1822 the whole of the Morea was in Greek hands, and deputies of the rebellious districts, meeting at Epidaurus, proclaimed the independence of the Greek nation. A National Assembly, presided over by Alexander Mavrokordatos voted the first Hellenic Constitution in euphoric recollection of the democracy of classical times. In savage revenge for their defeats, the Turks seized the island of Chios, where they perpetrated horrible cruelties on a defenceless people—23,000 inhabitants were killed and 47,000 carried off into slavery. Two daring Greek sailors, Canaris

and Miaoulis, set fire to the Turkish fleet in the roads at Chios and incurred the lasting gratitude of their people.

The situation was now transformed by the intervention of Egypt's powerful army and navy on the side of the Sultan. The brilliant but unscrupulous Mehemet Ali, an Albanian Muslim who had been in turn tax-gatherer, tobacco-merchant and commander of the Albanian contingent in the Ottoman army, had recently expelled the Turks from Egypt and set himself up as pasha there. He now offered his efficient army and navy to the Sultan for the suppression of the Greeks in exchange for the island of Crete and the provinces of Syria and Palestine.

Egyptian armies quickly overran the Morea while her fleets dominated the Aegean. European opinion was appalled to discover that hundreds of Greeks were being sold as slaves in the markets of Cairo, but the mutual rivalry between the powers and the belief that 'legitimate' governments

The Russian port of Sebastopol was bombarded ceaselessly by naval and land batteries.
Above: batteries in the camp of the Highland Brigade.
Right: inside the Russian fortress of Redan, which successfully resisted British attacks in 1855. (Bibliothèque Nationale, Paris.)

must be maintained at all costs prevented any joint action. Austria and Britain remained highly suspicious of Russian ambitions in the Balkans, and equally, Tsar Alexander had no wish to offend two such powerful nations.

Metternich commented at the Congress of Laibach in 1821, 'Over there, on the other side of our eastern frontiers, three or four hundred thousand people hanged, butchered, impaled . . . all that hardly matters. . . .' Not all accepted his counsel of despair. From all over Europe democrats and patriots flocked to the cause of Greek independence, inspired more by the vision of what had once been Greece than by the realities of the savage conflict. The French Colonel Fabvier offered his sword to the rebels, the great poet Byron joined Mavrokordatos at Missolonghi, only to die of fever two months later (1824).

Village by village, the Egyptian armies extinguished the flame of Greek independence. Missolonghi fell heroically in 1826, the last defenders setting fire to the powder-

kegs and blowing themselves up with their attackers: a year later Athens was forced to surrender. There remained in Greek hands only a few islands where the rebellion had begun six years before.

The intervention of the powers: Navarino

Unlike the issue of Italian independence, Greek independence ultimately succeeded because the European powers came to her aid. The invitation to intervene was made by George Canning, the British Foreign Secretary, who viewed Greece as the original home of European civilisation. France accepted out of sympathy, Russia because she also wished to win independence for her fellow Slavs in Serbia. Austria and Prussia were not interested in supporting a rebellion against a lawful authority, even if it were an authority as unworthy as that of the Turk.

In the Treaty of London (July 1827) Britain, France and Russia agreed to mount

a 'peaceful' naval blockade on Turkey which would force her, if negotiation failed, to recognise the rights of self-government of her Greek subjects. As the Turkish and Egyptian fleets, under the command of Ibrahim, son of Mehemet Ali, were at anchor in the roads of Navarino, the allied fleet drew near to make a show of strength. On 20 October 1827 what was intended as a naval manoeuvre erupted into war. A chance shot fired at the French flagship was taken to be a hostile act, and within a few hours of bitter fighting the Turkish and Egyptian fleets were destroyed. The Triple Alliance was now inevitably drawn into war by the outraged Sultan, and the politicians at home were forced to uphold the actions of their commanders in the field. The Greeks were to owe their freedom to the mistake of a Turkish sailor.

Charles X sent a strong French force to the Morea. Russian troops attacked in the Caucasus and on the Danube, while a British fleet was sent to Alexandria. By 1829 Russia had entered Adrianople, and the Sultan was

forced to sue for peace. The mixed motives of the allied intervention were demonstrated clearly enough in the peace settlement. By the Treaty of Adrianople (1829) Russia acquired strongholds in the Caucasus and Armenia, two ports on the Black Sea, and the right for her merchant ships to pass freely through the Straits of Bosphorus and trade with the Turkish Empire. The Sultan also recognised the independence of Serbia and of the Rumanian provinces Moldavia and Wallachia. The recognition of Greek independence came almost as an afterthought, and only partially, for the new state was not to include Thessaly or Crete and excluded many Greek-speaking peoples. In 1832 the crown of the little state was offered to a Bavarian prince, who became king of Greece as Otto I.

The issue of Greek independence, in itself relatively insignificant, was of profound importance for the future of Europe. It demonstrated on the one hand the chronic weakness of Turkey, 'the sick man of Europe', on the other the might and ambi-

tion of Russia for influence in the Balkans. It marked, too, the virtual end of the autocratic government of Europe by congress and Holy Alliance, as it did the increasing participation of Britain in the affairs of the Near East and in support of liberal movements generally.

The Egypt of Mehemet Ali

Mehemet Ali was by birth an Albanian, whose family had settled in Macedonia. He was working as a successful tobacco merchant when conscripted for military service in Egypt against the Napoleonic armies, where he showed great courage and daring. Having reached high office in the army, he had himself declared Pasha of Cairo by popular consent after the departure of the French. Now he gradually gained control over all the sources of power and wealth—the land, the army, commerce and trade. Ali was the classic example of the unscrupulous adventurer, clever, treacherous, always awake to the main chance and

his own advantage.

After establishing himself in Egypt he turned to a policy of expansion, seizing the holy cities of Mecca and Medina, conquering the Sudan and founding the city of Khartoum. The Egyptian army, manned mainly by Albanians, was made the most modern and efficient fighting force in the Near East, and it was typical of his Machiavellian way of conducting affairs that his method of expelling his Mameluke mercenaries was first to invite them to a banquet and then to have them put to the sword.

The more positive aspect of his policies lay in modernising the antiquated institutions of Egypt. Agricultural techniques were improved, cotton spinning and sugar refining industries established, harbours equipped and a modern merchant fleet founded. Foreigners were encouraged to bring Western knowledge to Egypt, and young Egyptians of promise were sent to study in London and Paris.

Above all, Mehemet Ali wished to legiti-

'*Crimea: a Crime.*' *The disastrous conduct of the war by the allies, and the absence of real cause for the conflict in the first place, has earned the Crimea the reputation of one of the most inglorious wars in history.*
In France, the government kept up public morale by disguising the truth about the real situation; '*Sanitary conditions in the army are excellent,*' *reported* Le Moniteur.
'*Dysentery has almost disappeared: there is no more trace of cholera. The mild temperature reminds one of the climate of Italy.*' *This was written in January, in the middle of the Russian winter.*
Above: bringing in timber to build huts.
Right: the relics of amateur warfare: two Rumanian soldiers in dress uniform.
(Bibliothèque Nationale, Paris.)

mise his rule, to make lawful the independence that he already possessed in fact. By 1830 he was sixty-one (Mehemet Ali, Napoleon and Wellington were all, by a strange chance, born in the same year) and needed to make his title hereditary so that it could pass to his son, Ibrahim. He also demanded Syria from Sultan Mahmud as the price of his military assistance against Greece and as compensation for the loss of his fleet at Navarino. When Turkey refused, Ibrahim invaded Syria in 1832, seizing Acre and Damascus and overrunning the Taurus.

The first Syrian War

Ibrahim's army decisively defeated the Turks, commanded by the Grand Vizier Pasha Rashid at Konieh. Again, the Sultan had to look for outside aid, and in desperation turned to the Russians who had so recently been his enemies: 'A drowning man clutches at a serpent', Mahmud is reported to have said. Again, the European powers became alarmed at the likely increase of Russian influence in the Balkans, and Britain, France and Austria all put pressure on the sultan to make concessions to Mehemet Ali and end the conflict; in the Treaty of Koutaieh (1833) Turkey agreed to cede Syria to the rebel. However, the Sultan also signed the secret Treaty of Unkiar-Skelessi with the tsar by which Russia guaranteed the safety of Turkish territory in return for the closure of the Dardanelles to all foreign ships. Under this agreement

the Black Sea would be virtually a Russian lake, denied to the trade of the world, and Russia would have established a practical protectorate over the Turkish Empire.

When the terms became known Britain felt her interests particularly threatened, and Palmerston, the Foreign Secretary, promised British aid for the reorganisation of the Sultan's armed forces: in return, he negotiated a trade agreement by which Turkey lowered her tariffs to a nominal amount. British forces were also permitted to occupy Aden, key to the Red Sea, to prevent further expansion of Mehemet Ali's power.

The second Syrian War

Under the aggressive leadership of Palmston, the British Foreign Office was now anxious to extend still further British influence in the Turkish Empire as a counterbalance to that of Russia. For his part, the sultan had never accepted the independence of Syria except under duress, and in 1839, encouraged by Britain, he sent a strong army against Ibrahim. It was crushingly defeated at the Battle of Nezib, while shortly afterwards, the Admiral of the Turkish fleet treacherously handed it over to the Egyptians.

Mahmud did not live to witness these tragedies. At the point of collapse, as it seemed, his empire passed into the hands of a seventeen-year-old boy, Abdul Medjid.

The new sultan had, at least, a sensible awareness of his country's failings and a genuine desire to reform. He began his reign by launching the *Tanzimat*, a programme of reform and modernisation which was to include a properly organised system of taxation and regular military recruitment: its good effect was, however, to some extent nullified by the apathy and reaction of the old guard.

It was Britain who now intervened to save Turkey from Mehemet Ali. Russia, Austria and Prussia were all in favour of a mediated settlement of the Eastern Question, France alone now supporting Ali. By the Treaty of London (1840) a ten-day ultimatum was delivered to him, under which he was to receive Egypt as a hereditary title and Palestine for life, but was to give up his other conquests and his fleet to the Sultan. This the pasha refused, supported by Louis Philippe and his minister Thiers. A leading French newspaper at the time declared, 'France should remember that, although alone in her position, she could resist the rest of Europe'. In the event, however, France was quite unprepared to take on a war against the three strongest powers of Europe. Palmerston, in a typical display of what has come to be known as 'gunboat diplomacy', sent a fleet and small expeditionary force to Syria, which was sufficient to persuade Mehemet Ali to submit. At the Conference of London (1841)

71

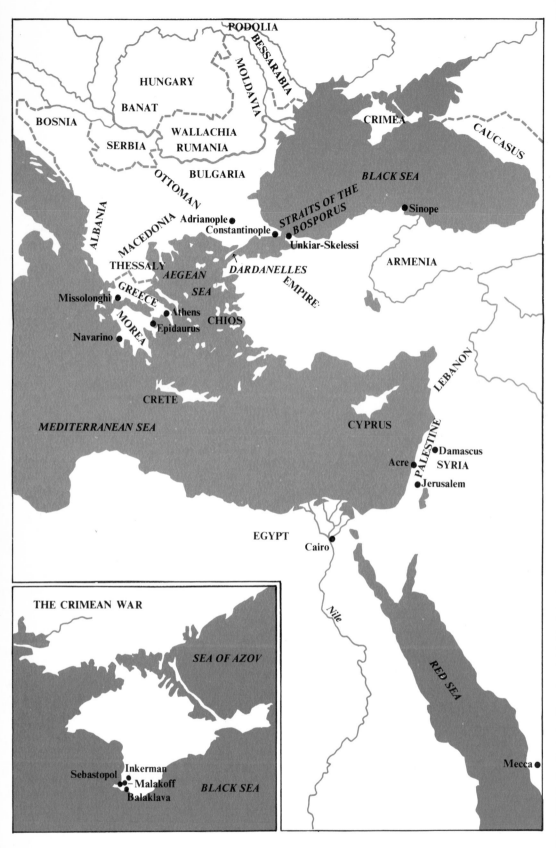

The 'Eastern Question' was the problem of the future status of those European territories controlled by the decaying Ottoman Empire during the nineteenth century. Disputes over these territories were largely responsible for the Crimean War (1853–56) between Russia and the allied powers of Turkey, England, France and Sardinia. The main result of the war was that Russia's influence in south-east Europe was checked.

Egyptian independence was ratified by the powers, subject to the payment of an annual tribute to the Sultan and a limitation on the size of the Egyptian army. Although his greater ambitions had failed, Mehemet Ali's original dream of establishing an Egyptian dynasty had been realised.

At the same time, the powers came to an agreement over the Black Sea in the Straits Convention, by which the Bosphorus and the Dardenelles were to be closed to the warships of all nations. This agreement, cancelling the terms of Unkiar-Skelessi, was a triumph for the British foreign secretary, Lord Palmerston, as was the Treaty of London as a whole. He had now prevented the future growth of the Egyptian army, halted the expansion of French influence in the Turkish Empire, and stopped Russia from converting the Black Sea into a private lake from which her warships could dominate the Eastern Mediterranean. In 1841, it seemed, the Eastern Question had been answered.

The dispute over the Holy Places

Under its new sultan the Ottoman Empire made some progress towards constitutional reform and the westernisation of her archaic institutions. Revolts in the Lebanon and in Bosnia were dealt with firmly but with clemency, and the vigorous application of the measures of the *Tanzimat* was beginning to bring progress to a country which had seemed rotten with decay.

A new and explosive crisis was, however, soon to develop. For centuries there had been dispute between the Greek Orthodox and the Roman Catholic churches as to which monks should have guardianship of the Holy Places in Jerusalem, Nazareth and Bethlehem. Historically, the Catholic monks had had custody, but in the seventeenth

Left: an advance post of the British army, to the west of Sebastopol. (Bibliothèque Nationale, Paris.)

century Orthodox monks had succeeded in ousting their rivals. On several subsequent occasions there had been open fighting between Greek pilgrims and Catholic monks, even in the Church of the Holy Sepulchre in Jerusalem.

In a sense, the problem of the Holy Places was a trivial ecclesiastical dispute which need never have grown to critical proportions. Turkey recognised that the great sanctuaries of the Christian world should be under Christian care, and to her it was a matter of indifference which sect was given that privilege. But political issues were inevitably involved in the dispute, since Russia regarded herself as the protector of the Greek Orthodox faith and Roman Catholics tended to look to France as theirs. During the Revolutionary and Napoleonic Wars France had been in no position to honour that role, but by 1850 there were good political reasons for the new government of Louis Napoleon to do so.

At the end of 1850 Louis Napoleon's government, anxious to win support from the French Catholics, made official protests about the custody of the Holy Places. Ali Pasha, the Turkish foreign minister, attempted to avoid offence to either side by establishing a mixed commission to try to reach agreement. As this did not satisfy anyone, it was very soon replaced by an all-Muslim commission. This eventually suggested a compromise by which Catholic monks were to hold the key of the main door of the church of Bethlehem, but not the right to hold divine service there, and a complicated arrangement by which the Christian sects were to follow each other in a kind of rota in the Sanctuary of the Holy Virgin. Such a solution was, of course, only likely to be productive of further quarrels in the future.

The 'Sick Man of Europe'

In a situation where the host country, Turkey, was unquestionably weak—some thought on the point of death—the policies and postures of the European powers were all-important. For her part, Russia had ambitions of southward expansion into the Balkans and control of the Black Sea; equally, Britain regarded this as a threat to her Eastern and Oriental interests. It was also significant that British public opinion, especially that part of it represented by the jingoistic policies of Palmerston, was strongly anti-Russian and regarded Nicholas I as evil, despotic and treacherous.

Nicholas believed, however, that he might reach an agreement with Britain, and it was in this hope that he declared to the British Ambassador, 'We have on our hands a sick man . . . let us reach an agreement to divide his inheritance'. He suggested that Britain should take Egypt to safeguard her route to India, and that Russia should receive Moldavia and Wallachia, Bulgaria and Constantinople, which would be made a free port. The moment for such a surgical operation seemed to the tsar opportune. France was on the point of re-establishing the empire after the *coup d'état* of December 1851, which gave Napoleon III dictatorial powers, and Austria was still feeling indebted to Russia for her help against Hungary in 1849.

Prince Menschikoff, the tsar's aide-de-camp, was sent to Constantinople with a demand for immediate satisfaction in Jerusalem and a treaty which would grant Russia a virtual protectorate over the 20,000,000 Orthodox subjects of the Sultan. Before replying, Abdul Medjid consulted the British ambassador to Turkey, Lord Stratford de Redcliffe, who was held in special respect as a known friend of Turkey and implacable enemy of Russia. In the event, Redcliffe

advised acceptance of the Tsar's demands, and throughout the negotiations, contrary to what was once thought, urged moderation on the sultan. Nevertheless, Medjid rejected Russia's demands, probably on the calculated risk that whatever the British ambassador was bound to advise officially, the British government could be relied on as an ally if necessary.

Britain and France continued to look for ways towards a negotiated peace, but in 1853 Russia occupied the principalities of Moldavia and Wallachia and Turkey gave an ultimatum for her withdrawal within one month. The first shots were exchanged between Russia and Turkey in October 1853, and a month later the Turkish fleet in the Black Sea was destroyed off Sinope. Russia's refusal to compromise had, it seemed, made war inevitable, and public opinion in Britain and France moved strongly in favour of early intervention on the side of the friendless Turk. In 1854 the two countries concluded a treaty of alliance with Turkey by which they agreed to defend Ottoman territory and not to seek any advantage for themselves. War with Russia was officially declared in March.

The Crimean War: Sebastopol

By the time that plans had been made and armies assembled Russia had already been driven out of Moldavia and Wallachia by Turkey unaided. The war was therefore conceived as principally a naval exercise, the point of attack being the great Russian naval base of Sebastopol in the Black Sea. A combined force of about 50,000 men was landed in September 1854 after the allies had won the Battle of the Alma, and encamped near Balaklava. Meanwhile Sebastopol had been heavily fortified, and resisted a long siege through the cold of the Russian winter. The necessity for the war—if 'necessity' it

had ever been—had now largely disappeared with the evacuation of the principalities. Why the particular target of Sebastopol was selected was never very clear, nor what strategic advantages would follow from its capture. It is likely that all that was in mind was some blow inflicted on Russian pride.

The Russians made two attempts to break through the allied lines—at Balaklava, where the Light Brigade was wiped out by the Russian guns, and at Inkerman, but cholera and frost-bite took far greater toll of the invaders than the enemy. The Crimean campaign soon became a public scandal for the gross inefficiency of its conduct, the mistakes of its military leaders and the neglect to ensure appropriate clothing, supplies and medical services for the troops. France had to recruit another 140,000 men for the campaign, while Piedmont supplied an expeditionary force of 15,000 so that she might take a place alongside the powers in any future disposition of European affairs.

A new general attack was launched in the summer of 1855, and in September a French division under General MacMahon at last succeeded in taking the fort of Malakoff and breaching the defences of Sebastopol. The city surrendered shortly afterwards, and the new tsar, Alexander II, was prepared to sue for peace. Though Palmerston, who had now become British prime minister, was in favour of a vigorous continuation of the war to some more dramatic victory, he was persuaded by Napoleon III that honour had now been fully satisfied and that a lasting peace in the Balkans could be made. 'The Empire is Peace' Napoleon had said on his accession. France had already lost 100,000 men in the Crimea, 85,000 of them killed by disease.

The Peace of Paris

The peace treaty, signed in March 1856, decreed that the Black Sea was to be neutral (neither Turkey nor Russia being allowed to maintain a war fleet there), that Moldavia and Wallachia were to be independent (Moldavia being enlarged by the addition of part of Bessarabia from Russia), that there should be free navigation of the Danube, and that Russia was to resign her protectorate over the Orthodox Church in Turkey. In return, the sultan promised to confirm the privileges of his Christian subjects.

The treaty thus secured for the allies all the aims for which they had professed to enter the war. For the time being, Russia was humiliated and crippled; France, for the first time since 1815, was restored to the rank of a great power; little Piedmont, represented by the brilliantly able Count Cavour at the conference table, was able to air publicly the wrongs of Italy at the hands of Austria. The empire of the Turk had been once more propped up, and the 'sick man's' illness halted, if not cured. Finally, the Treaty marked a considerable expansion of French influence in Turkey, evidenced by the establishment of a French lycée there and a considerable export of French capital.

In fact, the Peace of Paris solved none of the long term problems of the Balkans. By 1870 Russia had renounced the Black Sea clauses of the treaty, and the powers had acquiesced in her faithless act; Moldavia and Wallachia formed the independent kingdom of Rumania in 1866, so confirming the break-up of the Ottoman Empire which had been begun by Greece. Above all, Turkey remained weak and impotent, a prey to internal crises and to foreign ambitions which were to carry within them the seeds of the First World War.

Under the empire of Napoleon III France came to wield increasing influence in the affairs of the Near East. In 1854 a French engineer, Ferdinand de Lesseps, obtained permission to construct the Suez Canal. This painting by Kircher shows the visit of the Austrian emperor, Francis Joseph, to the inauguration in 1869. (Heeresgeschichtliches Museum, Vienna.)

Russia: the years of conflict

The December uprising of 1825; Nicholas I: an implacable enemy of liberalism;
reform and reaction under Alexander II; Tsarist Russia: a state ripe for revolution.

The period 1815–1870 also witnessed revolutionary changes in the eastern world no less far-reaching than those in the west. Russia, convulsed by her defeat in the Crimean War, passed from autocracy to a more liberal regime under Alexander II, who freed the serfs and established a process of modernisation and westernisation. When the forces he had unleashed seemed to be passing out of control, reaction returned and his reign ended in repression and terrorism. But despite her internal difficulties Russia. continued to pursue an expansionist foreign policy.

Russian history in this period is to a considerable extent the history of the tsars and the tsarinas who ruled the country with autocratic power: 'the people' seem shadowy, unsubstantial figures, moved here and there, like pawns, at the whim of rulers

and nobles. Under Peter the Great and Catherine II Russia had been brought into western political life, though no concessions had been made to those democratic ideas which exploded in France in 1789. On Catherine's death her son, Paul I, a mentally unbalanced tyrant, ruled for only five years until his assassination in 1801. With the accession of Alexander I hopes for reform revived. In particular, the tsar's minister, Speranski, was a great admirer of Napoleon and wished to introduce a representative system into Russia as a first step towards a constitutional monarchy.

Reaction and the Holy Alliance

But any progress towards liberalisation was soon dashed by the French invasion of

Russia in 1812. Napoleon and all that he stood for was now the arch enemy, and the Russian nation suddenly became united in a determined effort to repel the invader and resist the spread of subversive ideas. Speranski was sent into exile, and his enemies promoted to high office. One in particular, Arakcheyev, an extreme opponent of any change, was largely instrumental in turning Alexander's views from liberalism to autocracy. Under the influence too of the extremely pious and visionary Julie de Krüdener, the tsar became increasingly aloof from political life and inclined towards a well-meaning but vague form of mysticism.

Above: Alexander I of Russia (1801–25) in
army uniform. Painted by Daw.
(Pushkin Museum, Leningrad.)

It was in this spirit that, after the final victory of the allies in 1815, Alexander conceived the Holy Alliance—a union of nations which would preserve the peace of Europe in accordance with Christian principles. We have already seen how this well-intentioned scheme became an instrument for the suppression of all reformist movements, a mere buttress for the maintenance of despotism and privilege. In Russia itself the tsar's policy was now no less illiberal: students were forbidden to study abroad, foreign teachers dismissed, and all the apparatus of a police state was erected in an attempt to prevent any criticism of the government or its policies.

The Decembrists

In an unexpected and unintended way, however, the ideas of the French Revolution were to have profound effects in Russia. Russian armies had fought Napoleon in Europe and had been stationed in France after his defeat. Soldiers of all ranks returned to the homeland full of liberal ideas, convinced that Russian government and institutions were backward and corrupt. The effects of European culture and attitudes were most marked on the young officer class who despite the aristocratic origins of many, seemed suddenly to have developed a social conscience and genuine humanitarian instincts.

Freemasonry, illegalised during the reign of Cathrine II, was now revived and became a focus for liberal thought and discussion. Secret revolutionary societies multiplied throughout the country, including some of the highest nobility like Prince Paul Trubetskoi among their members. But such societies were mainly debating arenas for intellectuals, hardly action groups. Some advocated the establishment of constitutional monarchy, some a republic, others, like the United Slavs, a union of Slav peoples beyond the confines of Russia. Among the more extreme of the revolutionaries, how-

ever, some positive plans were being formulated. Men like Ryleiev and Colonel Pestel, son of a former chief of police, were among the strongest advocates of a republic, prepared even to assassinate the tsar and the royal family as the principal obstacles to their plans.

The death of Alexander I in 1825 posed a problem of succession, since the tsar left no direct heir. He chose to grant the crown to his second brother, Nicholas, but this was disputed by his elder brother, the Grand Duke Constantine. Ultimately, Constantine was persuaded to renounce his rights to the throne, but the whole occasion had provided an opportunity for the revolutionaries to take advantage of the uncertainty. On the morning of 14 December 1825, many officers who were members of the secret societies raised a body of troops in the belief that Constantine, who was being held prisoner in Warsaw, would not agree to a renunciation. The rebels formed up in Senate Square, St Petersburg, where the new tsar

Nicholas was to come to take his oath, but they were dealt with swiftly and efficiently. Artillery opened fire on the barricades, the rebels dispersed and arrests followed. The same pattern was repeated in the south, at Kiev, where loyal troops again suppressed the insurrectionaries. A trial of prisoners was carried out with apparent meticulous justice: 121 of the accused were brought before the High Court, where they defended themselves with great courage. Pestel declared at his trial, 'My greatest fault is to have tried to reap the harvest before I had sown the seed'. He and another were hanged, the rest of the conspirators being deported to Siberia.

Pestel's words were an apt comment on the failure of the Decembrists' rising as a whole. They had planned insufficiently, had counted on greater support from the people and had not imagined that so many of the troops would remain loyal to the tsar. But in one vital respect the rising of 1825 was significant. For the first time in Russian history members of the aristocracy had been allied with workers against the interests of their own class, and had been involved, not merely in a squabble over the succession, but in a fundamental attempt to change the nature of the state. The Decembrists left a legacy and an inspiration to future revolutionaries.

Autocracy and orthodoxy

For the thirty years of his reign Nicholas remained an implacable enemy of liberalism and the principal buttress of conservative ideas. He had come to the throne 'at the cost of the blood of my subjects', as he wrote to his brother Constantine, drawing from this experience a profound fear of any concession that might seem to encourage revolution. At the same time, he was acutely conscious of the responsibilities of his office, was hardworking and devotedly attached to the army and its iron discipline. These were hardly endearing qualities, and the new tsar's

Far left: Tsarina, Alexandra Feodorovna, daughter of King Frederick William III of Prussia.
Centre: Tsar Nicholas I, brother of Alexander, was an even fiercer opponent of liberalism: his reign opened with the stern repression of the December Revolution in 1825. (Pushkin Museum, Leningrad.)
Above: Alexander and his brother Constantine on the banks of the River Neva. (Peterhof, Leningrad.)

The rising of the Decembrists.
Below: on the 14 *December* 1825 *the rebels assembled in front of the statue of Peter the Great in Senate Square, St Petersburg. A water colour by Kolmann. (Pushkin Museum, Leningrad.)*

Right: loyal troops camp in the square, and the tsar, Nicholas, in the centre, is saluted by his officers. (Peterhof, Leningrad.)
Below right: the uprising was brutally repressed and there were numerous deportations. A water colour by Repin shows a group of chained prisoners awaiting deportation. (Pushkin Museum, Leningrad.)

regime quickly became a byword in the West for severity and inhumanity. De Tocqueville described it as 'the cornerstone of despotism in the world' and the Marquis de Custine in 1839 wrote that 'the Russian government has substituted the discipline of the camp for the order of the city: a state of siege has been made the usual state of society'.

Nor did the church escape the strict control of the government. A colonel of the Hussars was appointed to the holy synod (ecclesiastical assembly), and was given powers greater even than those of the patriarch, the nominal head of the Orthodox Church. The watchwords of the regime—'orthodoxy, autocracy, nationality'—were officially proclaimed by Count Uvarov, the minister of education.

The enforcement of such precepts required a ruthless and efficient police state, which effectively muzzled press and public opinion, banned secret societies, trade unions and all expressions of opposition to the state. An ardent nationalism and pride in Russia was to be impressed on the young, and it was in

keeping with this that foreign travel was made almost impossible, and French tutors and governesses—supposed sources of disaffection—placed under strict supervision.

There were, however, some more positive aspects of the Russian dictatorship. Speranski was recalled to complete the massive codification of Russian law which Nicholas's predecessors had begun, and in 1830 was issued the Complete Collection of the Laws of the Russian Empire which brought together into one code some thirty thousand legislative acts promulgated over the centuries.

Nicholas was also anxious to reorganise the cumbrous administration of the empire, and planned new central and local institutions which would bring greater efficiency into the archaic structure of Russian government. The only practical outcome of these plans was, however, the creation of a new government department—the tsar's 'personal chancery'—which was responsible among other things for the police régime. But Nicholas saw public order as the

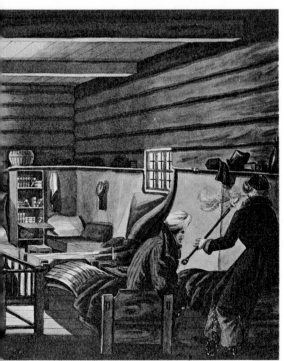

necessary condition of social progress. Once efficient government was established throughout his vast dominions, freedom and civil liberties could follow, the serfs could be emancipated from bondage and the subject peoples of the empire given control of their own affairs. Any hopes of such a gradual relaxation of policy were shattered by the revolution in France in 1830, and its repercussions in Russia, where the military garrisons in Novgorod rose in a revolt reminiscent of that of the Decembrists five years earlier. Although easily suppressed, the renewed threat of revolution brought to an end any move towards a more liberal policy.

In fact, Nicholas saw his greatest danger in the subject peoples who had been annexed to the empire after 1815—the Finns and Swedes of Finland, Germans, Estonians and Latvians in the Baltic provinces, the Poles, Lithuanians and Jews of Poland, the Georgians of Transcaucasia—none of whom had any sense of loyalty to the Russian crown and might be expected to seize any oppor-

tunity to shake off alien control. At the end of 1830, after revolutions in France, Belgium and Italy, the Poles rose in revolt, and the Grand Duke Constantine, military governor of Warsaw, was forced to flee, Polish officers and landowners fought bravely for a year against the might of Russia, inflicting and receiving heavy losses, but by September 1831 Warsaw had been subjugated and the rebels captured or dispersed. Thousands were exiled to Siberia and the last vestiges of Polish freedom were suppressed: for all practical purposes Poland disappeared, to be absorbed into the Tsarist empire.

The new Russia

But not even Russia could remain unaffected by the changes that were transforming western Europe. During Nicholas's reign Russia underwent the first stages of an industrial revolution, much of it necessarily initiated by the state in the absence of a sufficiently large and wealthy middle class. The tsar himself drew on a map with a ruler

79

the route of the railway line from St Petersburg to Moscow, work on which began after 1838, though no line yet connected Russia with the West. Much road development also took place, enabling the freer movement of goods and people. At the tsar's accession in 1825 Russia had 5,000 factories employing 200,000 workers: within ten years there were already 10,000 factories with 500,000 employees and economic growth was to continue apace. In her vast domains Russia had most of the raw materials necessary for industrialisation, while her large population provided at once a ready labour force and a potentially huge market. Already she was able to replace previously imported products, like textiles, with her own manufactures.

But, as elsewhere, industrialisation brought about social change and social problems. The growth of industry and trade offered opportunities for middle class manufacturers, merchants and professional people generally. Equally, it created a new urban working class alongside the serfs of rural Russia. Nicholas's deliberate policy was to encourage this new middle class and to ally it firmly to the monarchy. A class of 'notable citizens' was created with special privileges, who were to hold important positions in the civil service, commerce and the professions. But despite this development, significant for the future, Russia remained essentially a two-class society, with all real power monopolised in the hands of some 120,000 landed nobles. Russia was still a land of farms and villages and, with few exceptions, the towns were no more than overgrown market centres for the surrounding countryside, with wooden houses, unpaved streets and a total lack of sanitary provision. In 1838 there were 11,000,000 serfs, subject to laws which made them virtually the slaves of their lords, compared with a mere 80,000 free peasants, the numbers of whom grew only very slowly. Most lords continued to regard their serfs as chattels to be bought and sold, exchanged or pledged at the bank as security for a loan, brutally punished or imprisoned if they dared to offend. A police report of 1827 stated, 'the peasants await their liberation as the Jews await their Messiah'.

The tsars faced an impossible choice of policy—to modernise the institutions of Russia and so liberate forces which might overthrow their regime, or to try to maintain their autocracy in spite of the mounting pressure for change.

In particular, the promise of public education, made necessary by the increasing industrialisation of Russia as well as desirable on social and moral grounds, tended to whet the appetite for economic and political changes which the tsars were totally unwilling to concede. Nicholas's policy of limited and hesitant liberalism was to prove quite inadequate to resolve the country's problems.

Five of the rebels were condemned to
death, and more than a hundred deported
to Siberia.
Left: a panoramic view of the camp of
Petrovsk, where the prisoners were sent.
The picture was painted by one of them,
Abestuzhev.
Right: Maria Volonskaya, wife of one of
the 'Decembrists'. Through the window is
seen the prison of Shcheta. This was also
painted by Abestuzhev. (Pushkin Museum,
Leningrad.)

The intelligentsia

Leadership in the movement for the reorganisation of Russia now increasingly
passed to the intelligentsia of students
and teachers. As educational opportunities
widened some young men from the lower
classes began to find their way into university, and it was largely from such students,
inspired by German romantic philosophy,
that the revolutionary lead now came.
Contempt for riches and conventions, hatred
of tyranny and a somewhat mystical yearn-
ing for progress were its main characteristics,
though it was sometimes also mixed with a
strong sense of patriotism, the belief that the
Russians were a chosen people and should
go their own way independently of western
influences. Whatever their ideological differences, the intelligentsia were, however,
all agreed on one thing—that, as Herzen
expressed it—'the Slav race will take the
initiative in the Renaissance of humanity'.

These attitudes were clearly reflected in
the cultural developments of the new Russia.
Already the poet Alexander Pushkin (1799–
1837) had begun to free Russian literature
from classical and French influences, showing that English and German writers were
models more akin to Russian traditions:
another, Lermontov, wrote the epic *Heroes
of our Time* in a style closely similar to that
of Byron. During the reign of Alexander I
Pushkin wrote a number of what were soon
to become classic works—*The Prisoner of
the Caucasus, Eugene Onegin and Boris
Godunov.* But it was the work of a new writer,
Gogol, that marked a decisive turning-point
by using literature to take up a moral stand-
point. 'The writer,' he said, 'should make
judgments in the service of humanity,' and,
especially in his *Dead Souls*, he daringly attacked the shortcomings of Russian society
and administration. The same period also
saw the emergence of Ivan Turgenev, whose
masterpiece was *Fathers and Sons*.

The work which caused the greatest sen-
sation was, however, Nicholas Turgenev's
Russia and the Russians, published in France
in 1847 where the author had fled after the
December Revolution. The book was a bitter
denunciation of the evils of serfdom and the
vices of the tsarist regime. Such works had
a limited, and necessarily secret, circulation
among the Russian intelligentsia. With a
strict press censorship and police supervision they ran a terrible risk, and in 1849 all
the members of one political and literary
club—the Petrachevists—were arrested and
the leaders sentenced to death. As they stood
on the scaffold awaiting execution, the tsar's
pardon was proclaimed. The event left a
lasting impression on one of the condemned
men, Feodor Dostoevsky, who in *The Idiot*
described the mounting panic on the scaffold
and the cruelty of the delayed reprieve: the
nature of their offence had been officially
described as a 'conspiracy of ideas'. For this,
Dostoevsky was deported to a prison camp

in Siberia where he, appropriately, wrote his *Souvenirs from the House of the Dead.*

The Russian intellectuals of the 1840s were not revolutionaries thirsting for direct action against a corrupt state, so much as artists and idealists who used the political scene as the dramatic background for their canvas. But the intellectual ferment they created, and the public criticism that they levelled at the tsarist regime, was to take on a deeper significance in the next decade when the power and authority of Nicholas I was to suffer its first great defeat.

The consequences of the Crimean War

'War,' wrote Karl Marx, 'is the forcing-house of democracy.' In victorious Britain, the ineptitude of the conduct of the Crimean campaign brought reforms to the army and the civil service based on promotion by competition and ability in place of wealth and privilege. In defeated Russia, the consequences were even more far reaching. The Treaty of Paris, signed in 1856, marked, for the time being at least, the end of Russian ambitions of territorial expansion and the reversal of the steady growth of influence in Western affairs which had been built up for long centuries past. For thirty years Nicholas had been the greatest champion of counter-revolution in Europe, the arch-enemy of any change towards more liberal policies in the conduct of affairs. Dying at the beginning of 1855, he did not live to see the complete collapse of his system.

The Russian autocratic regime had been able to command the loyalty and submission of its subjects so long as it was militarily successful. Once defeated in the field, the faith in Russian supremacy which had silenced the voices of the critics was broken. The Crimea came as a shattering and traumatic experience to the armies which still rested on their laurels of 1812. To be beaten was bad enough, but to be beaten on her own soil by the two great liberal powers, France and Britain, assisted by the despised Turk, was catastrophe. The Crimean War was widely interpreted as a failure for autocracy, a success for liberalism. Russia experienced an agonised period of guilt and self-analysis, during which an outpouring of literature passed secretly from hand to hand, criticising all those who had been involved in the conduct of the war but, chiefly, the Tsar himself. 'Awake, oh Russia,' proclaimed one of the pamphlets; 'Awake from your long sleep of apathy and ignorance, Arise, prepare yourself, and demand before the despot's throne that he render account for the disaster that has befallen the nation.'

Alexander II and the abolition of serfdom

Nicholas had once said, 'My successor will do what he pleases: I myself cannot change.' In many respects it was the epitaph of the old regime. His son, Alexander II, came to the imperial throne at the age of thirty-seven, intelligent, tolerant, well-prepared for the role he was to play. In the manifesto in which he announced to the Russian people the end of the Crimean War Alexander stated that internal reform was necessary. A government which protected itself by silencing public opinion, a people of whom the majority were still bound by serfdom—such things were incompatible with a modern state, and largely explained the defeat of the armies in the field.

The key to reform was, however, to be gradualness. Little by little a greater degree of freedom was given to the press, the

Opposition to the tsarist regime was centred on the middle-class intelligentsia and revolutionary meetings were often held in fashionable salons.
Left: a salon in St Petersburg.
Below: the celebrated writer Alexander Pushkin sees his friend Kutelbacker, who had taken part in the December revolution, deported to a work-camp in Siberia in 1827.
Bottom left: the Nevsky Prospect, a famous street in St Petersburg, painted by Abestuzhev. (Pushkin Museum, Leningrad.)

universities and to public opinion in general. There was much discussion of the need for modernisation of Russian institutions along Western lines, of the development of railways, banks and industrial companies and of the improvement of education and agriculture. Pressure for change was kept up by Russian exiles, of whom the revolutionary leader and writer, Alexander Herzen in London was among the most outspoken in his journal *Kolokol* (*The Bell*).

Shortly after his accession the new tsar announced that he intended to emancipate the serfs, though not immediately. In fact, the problem was an exceedingly delicate one, and was examined in great detail by a Secret Committee for the Amelioration of the Situation of the Peasants, which was set up in 1857. Were the serfs to be freed with or without possession of their lands, and if granted land rights were they to have free possession or some kind of tenure? If, on

the other hand, emancipation was not to carry land with it, would it not merely weaken the position of the peasants, and possibly create a vast and dangerous rural proletariat?

Influenced by liberal advisers, Alexander II chose to grant freedom and land. Provincial land committees were established to investigate the problems locally and to report directly to the tsar who presided over the Central Committee. Alexander also toured the provinces personally, appealing for a spirit of generosity and conciliation among the great noble landowners. On 19 February 1861, the sixth anniversary of his accession, the tsar signed the manifesto announcing the greatest reform in Russian history.

By this bold measure, 47,000,000 peasants were granted personal liberty—21,000,000 the serfs of lords, 20,000,000 of the crown, and the rest a mixed body of servants and workers. The actual terms of the emancipation were, however, complex and not as generous as many had hoped. The peasants were granted freehold possession of their houses and the ground immediately surrounding; the farmland on which their livelihood depended was assigned to the collective ownership of the *mir* or village council, which then granted to the peasants the use of specific parts. A clear indication of the fact that the land was not his own was that the mir was charged with making a periodic redivision of the property, and even the mir was not the owner in the fullest sense since it was still subject to certain seignorial rights reserved by the lords. In fact, the reform satisfied no one. The lord, deprived of his forced labour, now had to hire workers or hand over all his estates to the mir. Equally, the peasant believed that the land he tilled should have become his, and felt cheated by any survival of the lord's authority.

During the reign of Nicholas I militarism invaded every aspect of Russian life. The tsar, who always appeared in military dress, himself designed uniforms for students and public officials.
Above: a military parade before the tsar and the royal court.
Right: the ceremony of changing the guard at the Winter Palace, St Petersburg. A painting by Ladurner. (Peterhof, Leningrad.)

Liberal reform

But in one respect at least, the institution of the mirs was an outstanding success. They introduced to the Russian people the idea of local self-government, free from the control of their former lords. They administered, judged and kept order on the democratic principle of equality in a society which had formerly been sharply divided into those who had rights and those who had none. The village mirs were grouped together into

larger units, the *volosts* (cantons), above which again were elected municipal corporations. Thus, the Russian peasants were given a complete system of local self-government, which ensured that, for the first time, the voices of the poorest and meanest of the tsar's subjects could be heard. In 1864 the same principle was extended to the major units of provincial administration, the districts and the provinces, which were given the right to elect councils (*zemstovs*) by universal suffrage and charged with responsibility for roads, schools, hospitals and provisions against famine. In these important regional assemblies the nobility were more strongly represented, yet nevertheless this new system of local government proved to be one of the main instruments bringing the nobility and the peasantry into contact and alliance with each other in the pursuance of common interests. The building of thousands of schools and the modernisation of agricultural techniques were two of their more important achievements. The growing number of towns also received a measure of self-government when the merchant corporations and craft guilds were allowed to elect representatives to the municipal council (*duma*). It seems, however, that Alexander was conscious of the possible dangers of allowing too much power to these democratic bodies. *Zemstovs* and *dumas* were never permitted to take joint action: the tsar was to remain the sole link between the two.

Another major reform, undertaken between 1862 and 1865, was the reorganisation of the system of justice. The courts were

increased in number and modelled on Western lines: juries were established, secret trials, torture and corporal punishment abolished. The most important principle was that the judiciary was to be separated from the executive arm of government, and so freed from royal control. As in the British constitution, the judges were to be independent, and able to arrive at their decisions without fear or favour.

In the early years of Alexander's reign a new spirit of freedom and conciliation seemed to be moving through Russia. The country which had once sought to suppress public opinion now seemed anxious to stimulate criticism and change. Press censorship was eased, control of the universities was relaxed, and many scholarships granted in order to spread higher education among those formerly excluded on the grounds of cost. To many it seemed that a new Russia, freer and greater than the old, was about to be born.

The young revolutionaries

The chief beneficiaries from these more enlightened policies were the intelligentsia and students, but far from drawing them into alliance with the tsar, the new taste of freedom served only to alienate them from his regime. In recognition of the growing danger, Alexander went back on some of his earlier reforms after 1861, for example by forbidding the universities to admit women or any student who could not subscribe to the orthodox religion. As the country began to take steps towards a more modern, indus-

The largest and most miserable part of the Russian population were the serfs, for whom Alexander II officially proclaimed the abolition of serfdom in 1861. In fact the reforms scarcely changed the lot of the peasant.
Far left: boatmen of the River Volga—some of the most oppressed of all the Russian serfs. A painting by Repin. (Historical Museum, Leningrad.)
Left: Tsar Alexander II, known as 'the Emancipator'. (Peterhof, Leningrad.)

trialised society, the social problems of the towns and their inhabitants increasingly forced themselves on the public's attention and the intellectuals turned for guidance and inspiration to the writings of the French socialists, and to Hegel, Marx and Engels.

Increasingly, the younger and more educated classes came to see revolution as the only means of creating a new world in which there would be no distinctions of rank or wealth, no nobles or serfs but a classless society in which each man could be free to give of his talents to the common good. This idealism was compounded of many elements—liberalism, socialism, not least, a devout religious faith which still inspired many young Russians as it had their fathers for generations before. Dostoevsky in *The Possessed* described the special atmosphere of mysticism which hung around the revolutionary intelligentsia. The organisation necessarily had to be secret, for despite his liberal sympathies, the Tsar could never have tolerated a body the whole object of which was aimed at the foundations of his power.

In 1861 Nikolai Chernychevsky, a publicist and critic, founded the most influential of these secret societies, 'Young Russia', which had the support of most of the intelligentsia and was in close contact with Russian émigrés abroad and with political prisoners exiled to Siberia. In the next year, Chernychevsky was himself arrested and deported to the prison camps, but others were soon willing to follow the lead he had given and in 1863 the society 'Land and Liberty' took up the struggle. In a climate of

opinion that now regarded any public criticism of the régime almost as treason, it was impossible that these dissentient elements could form a constitutional opposition party as they might have done in western Europe: their only recourse was direct action and terrorist activities against the state.

The hopes of the young Russian revolutionaries were raised by the growth of national feeling in Poland. Since the revolution of 1831 this poor country had suffered under the harsh yoke of Nicholas I who had tried to stamp out all vestiges of independence. But under the more liberal régime of Alexander II Polish hopes for political independence and for the recovery of the lost Lithuanian provinces revived. Increasingly 'Young Russia' saw the expression of its own hopes in the struggle of the oppressed Polish people.

The Polish insurrection

To the Polish people, the blunders and prevarications of the Russian government seemed a mockery. A strong nationalist spirit had persisted there ever since the abortive rising of 1831, strengthened by a fervent Catholic faith which further separated the Poles from the Russian Orthodox Church. The seeming impossiblity of any kind of peaceful negotiation with their Russian masters led, in the absence of any organised Polish army, to the outbreak of guerilla warfare in 1863. Within a short time fighting had spread to the whole country, and the Russian army was taking bitter reprisals against the civilian population, ostensibly for harbouring the rebels. Once again, the sympathy of the European powers was not translated into action. Abandoned to their fate, the Poles now lost all remnants of independence, and Russia was allowed officially to absorb the state into her dominions. By 1866 resistance had been

It was among middle-class intellectuals, found chiefly in the towns and cities, that opposition to the tsarist regime developed. Growing industrialisation and the use of modern techniques side by side with primitive agriculture made the Russia of the late nineteenth century a land of strange contrasts, of old and new, riches and poverty.
Top: Alexander Pushkin at his work table. A painting by Kontehalovsky.
Above: a street scene in St Petersburg. (Pushkin Museum, Leningrad.)
Right: Alexander II passing through a village in winter. The 'liberating tsar' was to be assassinated by bombs in 1881. (Peterhof, Leningrad.)

crushed: Russian was made the official language, and the former kingdom was carved up into ten regions forming part of the vast tsarist empire.

positive to offer in its place. Against this mounting opposition, the government of the tsar had two popular causes to offer—the unification of the unassimilated peoples of the empire, and the conquest of central Asia.

In the Caucasas, the primitive mountain people, Muslim in faith and owing allegiance to the Imam Schamyh, had resisted Russian advance for twenty years; they were finally defeated in 1859. Between 1865 and 1868 Turkistan, to the east, was overrun after the capture of Tashkent and Samarkand. Further east still, the crumbling Chinese empire was forced to cede the maritime province in which Russia founded Vladivostock, the 'key to the East' in 1860. For many people, the Russian despotism again seemed to be justified by its military success, though externally her expansion was watched with growing concern by Britain and, before long, by the new and ambitious power of Japan. Conquest alleviated but did not cure the ills of Russia.

The economic development of Russia

Terror and autocracy might, too, have been compensated by the material progress of the Russian people, by economic and industrial developments and a rising standard of living which might have brought a prosperity comparable to that which some western European countries were now enjoying. Russia was vast and populous, rich in material resources largely unexploited, and with a people noted for their hard work, their imagination and inventiveness. Precise statistics of the Russian economy in the 1860s are not available, but it is likely that at this time some ninety per cent of the people lived in villages, only ten per cent in towns. Russia was predominantly agricultural, with rather more than half her 260 million acres now in the hands of peasants. But the average size of holdings was only eight to nine acres per household, and many were too small to support a large family. The land was still divided up into tiny strips, often widely scattered, as it had been in Europe in the Middle Ages, one-third of it allowed to lie

Reaction in Russia

In effect, the Polish insurrection hindered rather than helped the liberal cause in Russia. Although hailed by some of the young revolutionaries as a bold blow for freedom, the more general reaction in Russia was to condemn the Poles as ungrateful rebels, and to rally public support solidly behind the government in its policy of 'pacification'. Liberal opinions, once tolerated and even encouraged, now came to be condemned as unpatriotic. The turning point in attitudes occurred in 1866 when a young student, Karakozov, unsuccessfully attempted to assassinate the tsar. The government was able to take advantage of the public alarm to put down all supposedly subversive movements. The members of the secret societies were tracked down and hundreds deported. The liberal experiment in Russia was at an end.

The 1860s therefore form a decisive decade in Russian affairs. A definite break

had occurred between liberal opinion and government policy: there could be no accommodation between the two, no steady progress towards a liberal constitution. From the time of Karakozov war was declared on the Tsar and all his policies, and terrorism became the order of the day. In 1881, fifteen years after the first attempt on his life, Alexander II died at the hands of an assassin.

The expansion of the Russian Empire

To some extent, the return of ruthless repression at home was compensated by a successful policy of expansion which helped to buttress the prestige of the tsarist regime. By the late 'sixties middle-class liberals had been alienated by the policy of stern despotism, and the more extreme revolutionaries had turned to the new philosophy of nihilism, a creed which challenged every aspect of the old order while having nothing

fallow and unproductive in each year.

The consequence of this was that modern methods of farming—the use of agricultural machinery, rotational systems and fertilisers —were almost unknown on most Russian farms. Even scythes, one of the simplest of all agricultural tools—had to be imported, and the primitive ploughs in use did little more than scratch the surface of the land. Despite the great fertility of her 'black earth' Russian wheat yields were only half those of Austria and France and one-third those of England.

The standard of living

Whether or not Alexander II's reforms produced any measurable change in the standard of life of the Russian peasant is doubtful. Just before the First World War the *Encyclopaedia Britannica* (eleventh edition 1910–11) commented:

'The present condition of the peasants—according to official documents—appears to be as follows. In the twelve central governments they grow, on average, sufficient rye-bread for only 200 days in the year—often for only 180 and 100 days. The peasantry are impoverished, and in many parts live on the verge of starvation for the greater part of the year.'

Although technically emancipated, the serfs were free only in name. They bore the brunt of Russian taxation, both direct and indirect, and were also taxed by the *zemstovs* on which they had only indirect represent-ation. For the most part they lived in huts of wood and mud with earthen floors and usually with no water supplies or sanitation: the single room was shared with pigs and poultry, and infectious diseases took a tremendous toll of human life. Even at the beginning of the twentieth century the Russian deathrate was the highest in Europe —thirty per thousand per year compared with sixteen per thousand in Britain—and one child in every three died during its first year. In 1914 only twenty-one per cent of the whole population could read and write, and the figure would have been smaller still in the 1860s. Count Witte, the prime minister in 1905–6, commented:

'The peasants are free from the slave-owners. But they are now slaves to arbitrary power, legal disabilities and to ignorance. The peasants have ceased to be private property. . . . That is all that remains of the reform of 19th February, 1861.'

Urban Russia

There was little more evidence of progress in the Russian towns than in the country-side. Although St Petersburg and Moscow were centres of culture and fashion for a few thousand nobles and rich bourgeois, the great majority of town dwellers lived in conditions no better than their country brothers. They were crowded into insanitary shacks and tenements and forced to labour at sweated trades, hardly yet affected by mechanisation, for a mere pittance. Rich material resources of coal and metals had scarcely begun to be exploited, and as late as 1914 only about one-tenth of the country had been geologically surveyed. Coal production was only one-twenty-seventh and iron-ore production only one-twelfth that of

90

Above left: street sellers and entertainers in Admiralty Square. Anonymous painting. (Historical Museum of Russia, Leningrad.)

Above: the Winter Palace, St Petersburg, painted by Sodovnikov. (Peterhof, Leningrad.)

the United States of America. This state of industrial backwardness was, to some extent, actively encouraged by the crown and nobility who feared the growth of a powerful urban proletariat as a possible source of change—even of revolution. Ultimately, as the events of 1917 were to demonstrate, their fears were amply justified.

Right: harvesters in the Russian steppes. A painting by Repin. (Historical Museum, Leningrad.)

FRANCE AND RUSSIA IN THE NINETEENTH CENTURY

	France	Russia	Other countries in Europe
1815	Restoration of Bourbons; Louis XVIII	Holy Alliance (1815)	Battle of Waterloo
	The Ultra-Royalists come to power	Nicholas I tsar (1825)	Holy Roman Empire becomes German Confederation under Austria
	The *Chambre introuvable*	The December uprising	
	The assassination of the Duke of Berry (1820)	Capture of Erivan (1827)	Uprising in Greece (1822)
	Expedition to Spain (1823)		Independence of Serbia
	Accession of Charles X (1824)		
	The Liberals are elected		
	The capture of Algiers and Oran		
1830			
	July Revolution in Paris	The Polish revolt (1830)	Independence of Belgium (1830)
	Louis Philippe becomes king	Russians take Vassorie (1831)	Victoria, queen of England (1837)
	Treaty with Abdul el-Kader (1834)	Treaty of Unkiar-Skelessi (1833)	
	Capture of Smala from Abdul el-Kader (1843)	Straits Convention (1841)	
	French Moroccan War (1844)		
1845			
	Affair of the Spanish marriages	Occupation of Danubian provinces	Revolutions in several countries (1848)
	Revolution in Paris (1848)	Start of Crimean War (1854)	Campaigns of Garibaldi in Italy
	Election of Louis Napoleon Bonaparte as president	Alexander II tsar (1855)	Crimean War (1854)
	Military expedition to Rome (1849)	Liberation of the serfs in the royal domain (1858)	
	Coup d'état of 2 December (1851)		
	The establishment of the Second Empire. (1852)		War between Austria and Sardinia (1859)
	An assassination attempt by Orsini (1858)		
	Franco-Sardinian alliance		
1860			
	Acquisition of Nice and Savoy	Emancipation of the serfs (1861)	Bismarck comes to power in Prussia
	Intervention in Mexico	Creation of the *zemstvos* (1864)	Sadowa—Prussia defeats Austria (1866)
	Liberal concessions (1867)	Attempted assassination of Alexander (1866)	Opening of the Suez Canal (1869)
	Ollivier ministry	Municipal reform	
	War against Prussia		
	Sedan		
	The fall of the empire		
1870			

France from the Restoration to Napoleon III

*The monarchy returns to France; Charles X and the causes of the 1830 revolution;
Louis Philippe, the 'citizen king'; the rise of republicanism brings Louis Napoleon
to power; France under the Second Empire.*

The French Revolution bequeathed to its
birthplace a heritage of problems—political,
social and economic—which successive
governments strove vainly to solve. To
reconcile liberty with order, to give effect
to the democratic principles for which
Frenchmen had fought while re-establishing
the necessary authority of the state, taxed
the energies and imaginations of statesmen
and politicians for more than half a century,
and to achieve this while at the same
time providing the conditions of economic
growth and military power ultimately
proved an impossibility. Monarchy, republic
and empire all fell victims to the same
enemies from within, and in this sense the
eventual consequence of the French Revolution was the humiliating defeat of French
arms on the battlefield of Sedan.

The restoration of the Bourbons

The last Bourbon king had fallen victim
to the guillotine. Now, in 1815, Louis XVIII
was restored to the throne, brought back
'in the baggage of the allies,' after more than
twenty years of exile. The new king was
intelligent enough to know that the *ancien
régime* could never be re-established, that
the middle classes were prepared to accept
a monarchy only if the essential freedoms of
the Revolution were confirmed. Thus at the
outset of his reign, Louis XVIII was brought
face-to-face with a fundamental philosophical problem which demanded immediate
and practical solution.

Although intelligent, cultured and refined,
Louis XVIII was ill-equipped to provide

such an answer. His long exile had taught
him to be patient and amenable and to
accept the position of a constitutional
monarch which was the condition of his
restoration: on the other hand, he had no
intention of playing only a nominal part in
affairs of state. Unfortunately, his closest
associates, led by his brother the Count of
Artois, were more royalist than he himself,

*Above: the first meeting between Louis
XVIII and the Duchess of Berry in the
forest of Fontainebleau, 1816. The Duchess
was exiled from France in 1830, but
returned in 1832 to try and win the French
throne for her son, the Count of Chambord.
Her intrigues ended in her imprisonment.
(Bibliothèque Nationale, Paris.)*

and were not prepared to make concessions to the principles of 1789.

Under the new constitution of 1815 the king was the head of state and the executive power: he had the right to chose his own ministers, who were not responsible to the parliament. The latter was to consist of two houses—an Upper Chamber nominated by the king, and a Chamber of Deputies chosen by an electorate limited to men over the age of thirty who paid at least 300 francs a year in taxes. There were less than 100,000 voters in all, and the working classes were totally excluded from political power. Moreover, even the 'democratic' Chamber of Deputies could only discuss legislation and vote taxes: since they had no executive power there was no means of enforcing their decisions unless the king also agreed.

Yet, despite its very limited nature, the constitution was regarded as revolutionary by many of the nobility and clergy who dreamed of a restoration of real power to the ancient pillars of the state. They had influential leaders like the Count of Artois

the Count of Villèle and the writer Chateaubriand, as well as their own organ in the *Gazette de France*.

Ranged against them were those who benefited from the new constitution—essentially the middle classes and professionals who had been brought into political competence, supported by a few enlightened nobles. These 'Constitutionalists' were led by the historian François Guizot, and expressed their views in the *Courrier Français*. To their left stood a more extreme group, led by Benjamin Constant and the veteran Marquis de Lafayette, who had no faith in the constitution and were uneasy at the excessive influence of emigrés and clergy in the new government. These 'Independents' drew most of their support from the lower middle classes: their objective was a more democratic constitution in which the elected chamber would have real power.

The restored government of Louis XVIII
owed its position to the backing of the allies
and its foundation was accompanied by a
wave of terror against former Bonapartists.
Left: the allies meeting at the Palais Royal,
Paris.
Bottom: Marshal Ney facing the firing
squad.

Right: an ironic drawing representing a
young Frenchman prematurely aged by the
effort of having to take the oath of
allegiance to so many different governments.
(Bibliothèque Nationale, Paris.)
Below: celebrating the restoration of the
Bourbons: a distribution of free food and
wine in the Champs Elysées, 1822. A
painting by L. L. Boilly. (Musée
Carnavalet, Paris.)

The *Chambre Introuvable*

One of the king's promises on his restoration had been an amnesty for all those Frenchmen who had supported Napoleon at the time of the Hundred Days, but in the country as a whole anti-republican feeling was running high. In several cities known Bonapartists were assassinated by mobs, and in the first post-war election the Ultra-Royalist party surprisingly won a majority in the Chamber of Deputies. Louis, who had not dared to hope for such support, described it as 'The Unknown Chamber'.

The king was now urged—probably not wholly against his will—into a policy of repressive conservatism. Talleyrand, the moderate prime minister, was replaced by the royalist Richelieu. Eighteen high-ranking officers who had fought with Napoleon at the end—including the once-popular hero Marshall Ney—were condemned and shot, while a general purge of the courts, the universities and local government removed some 9,000 from public office.

Finally, the Bonaparte family, and all those who had had any part in the execution of Louis XVI, were banished from France.

But if the royalists wished to restore the *ancien régime*, the king knew that to do so would lose him his crown. Making an astute appraisal of the political feeling of the country, Louis dismissed the chamber in September 1816 and held another election in which the Royalists lost many seats and the Constitutionalists gained a small majority. For the next four years France was to experiment with more liberal policies.

The constitutionalists in power

The old king now had an opportunity to show his wisdom and shrewdness in steering a middle course between the two extremes of reaction and reform. Though he never became a popular figure—the memories of France's departed glories and the bitter pangs of Waterloo were too strong for that —he succeeded ably in maintaining peace

and prosperity while paying off the country's war indemnity and liberating her soil from foreign armies. Under the new prime minister, Décazes, the electoral law was altered in order to reduce the influence of the great landowners over their tenant voters, military conscription was replaced by a volunteer army of a quarter of a million and, again to reduce aristocratic power, officers were to be selected by competitive examination and promoted by seniority and merit. Finally, in 1819, press censorship was abolished, and in future cases concerning publications were to be tried by jury in the assize courts, no longer by special tribunals appointed by the government.

One of the unforeseen results of this general relaxation of control was a large increase in the circulation of liberal newspapers, and in the 1819 elections the Independents gained considerable ground. Decazes, alarmed at the strength of the forces he had unleashed, brought his programme of reforms to an end, dismissed several of his most liberal ministers, and increasingly allied himself with the Right. Groups of extreme anti-clericals had associated themselves into secret societies on the model of the Italian *Carbonari*, and in 1820, when there were revolutionary outbreaks in Piedmont, Naples, Spain and Portugal, there were disturbances in France which culminated in the murder of the king's nephew, the Duke of Berry, by a Bonapartist fanatic. Under pressure from his own family and the country, Louis dismissed his friend Decazes. The Ultra-Royalists quickly seized power in the council, appointing one of their own number, the Count of Villèle, as president.

Villèle and the reaction

There now followed the undoing of much of Decazes patient reconstruction. Villèle, the puny little member for Toylouse, was a shrewd administrator who understood clearly enough the realities of political power. In order to halt the progress of the liberals he abolished the new electoral law and, moreover, introduced double voting rights for that quarter of the electors who paid the most taxes: political competence was to rest upon economic foundations, not on abstract principles of justice and equality. As a result, the liberals lost heavily in the elections of 1820, and Villèle completed their defeat by reimposing censorship of the press and the hearing of cases by special tribunals: in this way the publication of most opposition journals was stopped.

Left: the assassination of the Duke of Berry, the king's nephew, in 1820, as he was leaving the opera in Paris. The Ultra-Royalists took advantage of the event to seize power and end the liberal experiment of Decazes.
Right: a caricature of 'The Knights of the Weathercock'—those politicians who quickly altered their opinions each time the winds changed. (Bibliothèque Nationale, Paris.)

Villèle's policies relied in part on a renewed energy and spirit in the Roman Catholic Church, which through a determined onslaught on the schools and universities was attempting to reconquer areas of French life which had lapsed into paganism during the Revolution and subsequent war. Villèle strongly supported the *Congregation*, an association dominated by the Jesuits, and placed the universities under the supervision of the bishops.

But despite the attacks on them, the opposition continued a vocal criticism of the government and its policies. The fifteen members of the left in the Chamber of Deputies included some outstanding orators like Benjamin Constant and General Foy, while secret presses continued to pour out broadsheets and songs denouncing the government and the Jesuits. In the univer-

sities student demonstrations against control by the Church were often violent, especially when popular professors like Guizot and Victor Cousin were suspended from their duties.

Among some of the more extreme revolutionaries the belief grew that Villèle's regime could only be ended by armed insurrection. Republicans like Lafayette and Cousin formed secret *Charbonneries* with cells of twenty members directed by a high command. Badly organised and idealistic, they were no more successful than their Italian counterparts, and had little support from the public at large. The ease with which their local risings were put down indicated that the government had the situation well in hand, and that they constituted no real threat to the authority of the Ultras. But in September 1824 the old king died and was

succeeded by his brother, Charles X, who in a few months was to destroy what little credit the French crown had left.

Charles X: from Villèle to Polignac

Where Louis had been shrewd, moderate and easy-going, Charles was unintelligent, stern and autocratic. At sixty-seven he was the epitome of the *ancien régime*, proud, haughty and unbending, a staunch adherent of the Church and an implacable enemy of paganism and reform. 'I had rather chop wood,' he had once said, 'than reign after the fashion of the King of England,' and his coronation ceremony was symbolically performed at Rheims with the full pageantry of medieval rites. One of his first acts was to increase the penalties for sacrilege, and it

rapidly became clear that Charles intended
to put the clock back to 1789. His abolition
of the National Guard, who had demonstrated in favour of constitutional reform,
and his granting of compensation to the
émigré nobles, were especially unpopular.
In the Chamber, Constitutionalists and
Liberals allied together in a powerful opposition headed by Guizot, and in the next
elections won a majority of 250 seats against
the government's 200. Villèle had no alternative but to give his resignation to the king
in January 1828.

Charles was now faced with an unmange-
able Chamber and a seemingly impossible
situation. To gain time, he first appointed
a Constitutionalist, Martignac, who com-
pletely failed to win the support of the
deputies. Increasingly, the feeling grew that
the king was planning a *coup d'état* to
overthrow the constitution and restore the
ancien régime. This view seemed to be confirmed the following year when he dismissed
Martignac and appointed Prince Polignac,
one of the original émigrés and a man who
had refused to swear allegiance to the
Charter of 1815: one of his stranger delu-
sions was that he received direct guidance
from the Virgin Mary.

The glorious days of 1830

The political crisis of 1829 had resulted
in important regroupings of the parties, the
Republicans growing in strength but, more
important, a new party led by the Duke of
Orléans, emerging into the forefront of
affairs. This was a party of moderate Royalists, anxious to safeguard the interests of the
middle classes and having the support of
influential men like Talleyrand and Adolphe
Thiers. Their ideal was a constitutional
monarchy like that of England, where power
was shared between the sovereign and the
houses of parliament.

Faced with growing opposition in the
Chamber of Deputies, Polignac now dismissed parliament and prepared for an open
conflict. On 25 July 1830, royal ordinances
were issued which limited the freedom of the
press, dissolved the Chambers and altered
the electoral law. Although the king had
authority under Article 14 of the Charter to
do so, it was clearly a provocative gesture,
especially as the new electoral law limited
the franchise to those who paid land tax or
property tax and so deliberately excluded
many professional and businessmen who
were known liberal supporters.

It was the journalists who reacted first,
on 26 July, by issuing a declaration that they
would continue to publish newspapers without the required permission.

Next day, workers from the poorer
quarters of Paris erected barricades in the
streets, but the final spark to the revolution
was given on the 28th, when the government
announced that the hated General Marmont, who had betrayed Napoleon in 1814,

98

had been given command of the royal armies. There followed three days of disorder and fighting, when thousands of Parisians of all classes marched through the streets with tricolour flags at their head. Students of the Polytechnic had previously seized several army barracks and distributed arms to the population. Those royal regiments which had not gone over to the rebels were quickly overcome, and after the capture of the Louvre and the Tuileries, Marmont, defeated, evacuated the capital.

The victory of the Orleanists

The revolution of 1830 was over before most French people realised what was happening. The events had happened entirely in Paris, so that the royalist strongholds in the provinces were unable to move until it was too late. But in some ways, the strangest part of the revolution was its outcome. Its leaders had been mainly Republicans or Bonapartists, anxious to establish in France either a presidential constitution or a second empire under one of the children of Napoleon. In fact, the result was neither of these, but a bourgeois monarchy under Louis Philippe, the head of the House of Orléans, who as a young man had fought in the revolutionary armies and had subsequently known sorrow and poverty. The Orléanists, essentially the party of the middle classes and professionals, were able to turn events to their advantage partly because they were better organised than their political opponents, and partly because a constitutional

monarch who would accept the Chamber and honour the tricolor represented a middle way which the majority of French people could support. It was therefore relatively easy to persuade the two Chambers, on 30 July, to send a deputation to Louis Philippe offering him the crown, in much the same way that William of Orange had been invited to take the English throne in 1688. The Parisian mob, at first somewhat hostile, were won over when Louis Philippe appeared on the balcony of the Hôtel de Ville, draped in a tricolour flag, and warmly embracing Lafayette, 'the grand old man of the revolution', who had announced his adherence to the Orléanists.

Meanwhile, Charles X made a last bid to rescue the situation for the Bourbon dynasty, abdicating in favour of his young grandson the Duke of Bordeaux, and suggesting that Louis Philippe should act as Regent until he came of age. This Louis refused, and after further threatened attacks by the Paris mob, Charles escaped to England. The throne of France was officially offered to Louis Philippe by the two Chambers on 9 August.

The July Monarchy

There could hardly have been a greater contrast between the new king and his Bourbon predecessors. To outward appearances he was the personification of the petty bourgeois—a shabbily dressed man who loved to stroll through the streets of Paris with his umbrella under his arm, a devoted

The beginning of the 'bourgeois revolution'.
Left: on 28 July 1830, Parisians marched on the royal palace of the Tuileries, despite heavy fire on the bridges. General Marmont and his army of 8,000 men were forced to evacuate by the next day.
Above left: the capture of the Hôtel de Ville by the Parisians.
Far left: the taking of the Louvre on 29 July. A painting by J. L. Bezard. (Bibliothèque Nationale, Paris.)

father of five sons and three daughters, a man of simple tastes and no pretentions. Behind this very ordinary exterior there also lay much courage and resolution, a sound business sense and a determination to raise the authority of France from the low levels to which Charles X had reduced it.

Louis Philippe accepted a constitution considerably more democratic than that of 1815. By a series of amendments, the king no longer had the power to promulgate ordinances having the force of law, press censorship and double voting were abolished, and in future the choice of prime minister was to lie with the two Chambers. Thus parliamentary supremacy over the legislative function was clearly and absolutely established. By additional clauses, the National Guard was permitted to choose its own officers, the hereditary peerage was abolished and the Chamber of Peers opened to the middle classes, and the property qualification for the vote in the Chamber of Deputies was lowered from those paying taxes of 300 francs a year to 200 francs. By this last, the electorate was doubled to include 200,000 citizens.

The new king's policy was clearly to try to steer a middle course between the two extremist groups, the Republicans and the Bonapartists. Like all compromises, it satisfied few people. The Republicans regrouped under the leadership of such men as Carrel, the lawyer Garnier-Pagès and the chemist Raspail, and through the now free press launched a campaign for universal suffrage. Again secret societies sprang up to prepare the ground for the next general election. Even within the Orléanist party, differences of opinion appeared between the more conservative leaders like Casimir Périer and Guizot, who believed that reform had now gone far enough, and liberals like Laffitte and Lafayette who wished to continue reform towards an even more democratic constitution. Louis Philippe had to choose between the two: he chose the liberals under the leadership of Laffitte, 'the king of bankers and the banker of kings'.

The revolt of the silk workers

One of Laffitte's immediate problems was the trial of Charles X's former ministers. Justice seemed to require that they should be punished for the injuries they had inflicted on the French people: the more extreme elements demanded their execution, the upper house contented itself with sentencing them to life imprisonment. Widespread demonstrations had accompanied the trial, and early in 1831 there was a wave of violent anti-clericalism when Roman Catholic priests were insulted and attacked. In an attempt to win popularity, Laffitte lowered the taxes on alcoholic drinks which only had the result of producing a budget deficit of forty million francs.

Louis realised that the situation demanded

Above: a view of the Ile de la Cité and the Pont Neuf in Paris, 1832. A painting by Giuseppe Canella. (Musée Carnavalet, Paris.)
Above left: Louis Philippe of Orléans, the 'bourgeois king'. A portrait of the young Louis by L. Cogniet. (Musée de Blérancourt.)
Below left: street fighting in Paris in 1830, showing how the ordinary citizens gave their support to the rebels. (Bibliothèque Nationale, Paris.)
Right: the battle of the rue de Rohan, 29 July 1830. A painting by H. Lecomte. (Bibliothèque Nationale, Paris.)

Above: Louis Philippe, Duke of Orléans signing the proclamation by which he accepted the throne of France at the Palais Royal, 31 July 1830. A painting by J. D. Court.

Right: the Chamber of Deputies presenting Louis Philippe with the Act which called him to the throne and the Charter of 1830. A painting by F. Heim.
Below: the presentation of colours to the National Guard by Louis Philippe at the Champs de Mars, August 1830. A painting by Dubois. (Musée de Versailles.)

of a further 300 rebels in Lyons. Such risings could be put down with relative ease because the army remained loyal and because the National Guard, an essentially middle class body, could always be relied on for support, but they demonstrated an inherent weakness in Louis Philippe's regime that it was not firmly based on the respect and affection of all classes of Frenchmen.

In 1835 an attempt on Louis' life served as the pretext for laws directly aimed at the Republicans. One imposed severe penalties for spoken or written attacks on the monarch, including the caricatures of Louis Philippe by Honoré Daumier and other artists which had been circulating; the other officially outlawed Republicanism and laid down special rules for the trial of political offences.

Within about four years, therefore, Louis Philippe's government, now under the leadership of conservatives like Guizot and Thiers, had brought the liberal experiment to an end but, at least, had established firm government. For the time being, the Republican menace was halted, both in the Chamber of Deputies and in the country at large, and for a few years France was to enjoy a period of calm during which economic expansion and a growth in prosperity seemed to justify the political conservatism of the July Monarchy.

The ministry of Guizot

For some years after 1835 Louis Philippe virtually ruled France himself. Technically, a series of puppet ministers presided in the Chamber, and the middle classes, enjoying a period of unusual economic growth and prosperity, were for a while content to allow him to hold the reins of power. In the elections of 1839, however, the prime minister Molé, was defeated, and after some months of hesitation, Louis gave the leadership to Guizot, a distinguished academic historian who, in politics, was a staunch royalist and conservative. To Guizot the constitution of 1830 was perfect: the art of the politician was to make it work, to give the monarch a position of real influence in government while allying the representatives of middle class wealth and culture solidly behind the throne.

But the first task of any government, Guizot believed, was to maintain order. He inherited a confused situation in which Republican and dissident elements, secret societies and subversive literature constituted a serious threat to public order and to France's economic development, and in the very year of his taking office 700 rebels belonging to one of the secret societies known as 'The Seasons' occupied the law courts and the police headquarters in Paris. Precisely what they intended to do is not clear, though it seems that they hoped to overthrow the constitution and establish a republic. Guizot's new government dealt

---

a firmer hand. Dismissing Laffitte, he appointed Casimir Périer, another banker but an authoritarian of more conservative views, determined to suppress public disorder. Within a few months the budget was again balanced and the new minister could turn his attention to a serious situation which had appeared in Lyons, the centre of the great French silk industry. In November 1831 the weavers, wretchedly paid and housed in miserable slums, had taken up arms against their employers, and had occupied the town after two days of bloody fighting against the police and the army. Whatever the rights or wrongs of the situation, Louis Philippe's government could not allow such a threat to public law and order to continue, and General Soult was ordered to march on the city.

The army regained possession of the city on 5 December, the silk workers then being disarmed and treated as rebels: if anything, their conditions subsequently grew even worse. It was thus clearly demonstrated, early in the new reign, that the rights of the property-owning middle classes were to be regarded as paramount, and that the Revo-

lution of 1830 had served merely to confirm the power of the bourgeoisie while leaving the workers as excluded from political participation as they had been under the Bourbons.

The republican opposition

The stirrings of the Lyons proletariat had hardly been suppressed when a new threat to the monarchy appeared. In 1832 the Duchess of Berry, widow of the murdered Duke and mother of Prince Henry, the heir of Charles X, landed in the Vendée, western France, in an attempt to rally support for her son's cause. In the event, she drew few followers, and was arrested shortly afterwards in Nantes. At least the episode demonstrated that royalist opposition to Louis Philippe was no longer a serious threat.

More disturbing was the growth of the Republican movement. In June 1832 there was a serious rising of Republicans against the government, when over 800 died in bloody street fighting. Two years later another insurrection, inspired by the Society for the Rights of Man, resulted in the deaths

RÉPUBLIQUE FRANÇAISE.

Combat du peuple parisien dans les journées des 22, 23 et 24 Février 1848.

with them easily and effectively, surrounding the rebels and arresting the leaders, Barbès and Blanqui, yet the episode demonstrated the continued and growing attraction which the idea of a republic had for many Frenchmen.

The other strong current of opposition opinion was Bonapartism. As the years went by, the tyranny and oppression of the empire was forgotten, only its glorious victories before which the powers of Europe had trembled were remembered. Poets, historians and pamphleteers combined to venerate the Little Emperor, to reinterpret his defeat during 'The Hundred Days', and to record his reminiscences and conversations from his exile in St Helena. It was symbolical of this process of rehabilitation that in 1840 his ashes were brought back from St Helena to be given honourable burial at Les Invalides in Paris, the funeral carriage being followed by an immense crowd. As yet, it was too soon for the Bonapartists to overthrow the strong government of Louis Philippe.

The head of the Napoleonic house was Louis Bonaparte, nephew of the great Napoleon and son of Napoleon's brother who had once held the throne of Holland.

He was a strange, studious young man, convinced of his imperial destiny and unabashed by the utter failure so far of his attempts to seize power in France. Already in 1834 he had unsuccessfully tried to win over the garrison of Strasbourg. Now in 1840 when he landed at Boulogne the French army, instead of rallying to his cause, merely captured and imprisoned him in the fortress of Ham. Yet, in retrospect, the origins of the Second Empire are discernible plainly enough in the events of 1840.

For the next six years Guizot's conservative ministry continued to resist all political change. Industry and agriculture prospered, and in 1842 plans were drawn up for the construction of a huge railway network converging on Paris. The philosophy of 'grow rich, pay taxes, and you too will enjoy the vote' gradually brought a few more Frenchmen into democratic competence, and in the elections of 1846 the government was overwhelmingly returned to power. In all outward appearances at least 'the bourgeois king' was more secure than at any time since his accession.

The revolution of 1848

The beginning of the trouble was an economic crisis, caused by a failure in the wheat and potato harvests in the autumn of 1846. As prices soared, bands of starving people began looting the bakeries, spreading terror throughout the countryside, while in the towns factories closed and the numbers of unemployed multiplied alarmingly. At the same time, the disclosure of a series of government scandals gave the opposition their opportunity to demand changes in the electoral system and the lowering of the property qualifications for the franchise to 100 francs. Unwisely, but predictably, Guizot refused all pressure for change. The opposition leaders now decided to put the issues before the public, organising mass meetings at which they exposed the government's failures to large and enthusiastic audiences of workers. Republicans like the journalist Louis Blanc and the author Alphonse de Lamartine quickly came to the forefront, campaigning for universal suffrage and the improvement of economic conditions.

'The wind of revolution is blowing'

Contemporary prints of the street fighting in Paris during the revolution of 1848.
Far left: 'The French Republic: the struggle of the people of Paris throughout the days of 22–24 February 1848.'
Left: 'Fire if you dare: it is the flag of France'.
Below: 'The massacre at the Ministry of Foreign Affairs. The crowd on the boulevard was in a happy mood, hoping that reform could now come without more fighting, when shots suddenly rang out and fifty people lay dead.' (Bibliothèque Nationale, Paris.) These scenes illustrate the violence of the street fighting, despite the fact that soldiers often refused to fire on the crowd.

Paris, Codoni r. Grenetat 18.   Lith. Veyron

MASSACRE DU MINISTÈRE DES AFFAIRES ÉTRANGÈRES.

Une foule nombreuse se promenait sur les boulevards dans la joie et l'espoir d'obtenir sans plus de combat une réforme lorsque tout à coup une décharge se fait entendre 50 personnes venaient d'être tuées

Top: the insurrection at Lyons, led by the Republican Society for the Rights of Man, April 1834. (Bibliothèque Nationale, Paris.)

Above: one of the many caricature-portraits of François Guizot, the French statesman and historian. (Bibliothèque Nationale, Paris.)

Above right: the remains of Napoleon Bonaparte, brought back to France from St Helena in 1840 for state burial at the Invalides. Painting by V. Adam. (Musée Carnavalet.)

wrote de Tocqueville. The storm burst on 22 February 1848, when Guizot refused permission for a public banquet being given by the Republicans. A protest demonstration turned into a riot when a frightened army patrol fired a chance volley into the crowd. By the 23rd the National Guard had joined the rebels and Louis Philippe's dismissal of Guizot came too late to retrieve the situation. As in 1830, arms were seized from the barracks and barricades erected in the streets, but, as in 1789, it was the 'Marseillaise' that was on everyone's lips. After some skirmishes with the remaining royal troops the crowd marched to the Tuileries where Louis, abandoned by all, abdicated and shortly afterwards fled to England.

The speed and easy success of the revolution startled even the Republicans. Their problem now was to make sure that the victory was not wrested from them, and to do this meant excluding the deputies from any share in the success. The crowd took possession of the Chamber, Lamartine read-

ing out the names of the new government to the Parisians who crowded into the benches and galleries. The Republic was then officially proclaimed from the Hôtel de Ville.

The two flags

Louis Philippe's government had given France for eighteen years an unaccustomed measure of peace and prosperity, but it ultimately failed because it was not broadly based on the popular will. By devoting itself to the avarice of the middle classes it had alienated that growing body of workers on whom the wealth of France depended, and they, in anger and despair, had ended the life of a monarchy which had either treated them with contempt or ignored their very existence. Now these same workers were flushed with success, but unorganised, inarticulate, an easy prey to the demagogue who could promise all.

At the same time as Lamartine was proclaiming the new Republic, another group had strong supporters in the crowd. These

were the socialists, followers of Louis Blanc and Albert, who had derived their ideas from earlier French philosophers like Saint-Simon, Fourier and Proudhon, and were now advocating fundamental economic, not merely political, changes. At the meeting at the Hôtel de Ville they had tried to substitute the red flag of socialism for the tricolour of the republicans, but Lamartine had rushed forward and, in a famous speech, had condemned their emblem as the flag of blood and hatred. He was not, however, able to prevent the inclusion of the socialist leaders in the new government.

The Republicans knew clearly enough that the immediate cause of the revolution had been the economic crisis and the miserable poverty of many of the working classes, but even if they had wanted to exclude the proletariat from power there was no way of doing so. Universal suffrage which had been proclaimed would now enfranchise nine million people instead of a quarter of a million. Freedom of the press and of public

assembly resulted in the appearance of hundreds of revolutionary newspapers and political clubs. For the first time, it seemed, a new working class consciousness had emerged, in which they were no longer content to accept the leadership of middle class liberals but wanted a complete reconstruction of society on their own terms. To outside observers like Marx and Engels, publishing their Communist Manifesto at this time, it seemed that the hour of the proletarian revolution had struck.

In the uneasy situation the new government played for time, appointing a special commission to enquire into working conditions in industry which resulted in a substantial reduction of hours. But there were growing signs of a rift between the middle classes and the socialists over the timing of the general election, the one urging delay, the other pressing for immediate action. Popular discontent was further heightened by increases in taxation made necessary by the government's critical financial position.

The April elections

In fact, the postponement of the elections favoured the Socialists rather than the Republicans. Lamartine and his followers believed that people instinctively recognised the truth when it was presented to them, and that propaganda was therefore wasted on intelligent and discriminating human beings. More realistically, the Socialists knew that many of the French working classes were poor and illiterate, and believed that they were entitled to a period of instruction to remedy the effects of their political inexperience. Demonstrations and mass meetings were therefore organised throughout France, sometimes attended by as many as 100,000 to listen to renowned speakers like Louis Blanc. On some of these occasions public order was only kept by the National Guard, and a growing rift became apparent between the two groups who had so recently been allied to bring about the revolution.

On 23 April for the first time millions of

Frenchmen went to the polls. The results were as the Socialists had feared. France was still a predominantly rural country, and the strength of socialism was almost entirely among the exploited working classes of the towns. The peasant was traditional and conservative in outlook, a staunch supporter of property and order, and suspicious of the Parisian trouble-makers. The newly-elected Assembly was moderate and middle class, hardly dissimilar from that of Louis Philippe's closing years. Of 900 Deputies only 100 were Socialists, fewer than the 130 Royalists of the extreme right: the rest were moderate Republicans, pledged to suppress disorder and to restore financial stability to France.

The National Workshops

The first general election to be held under conditions approaching manhood suffrage was, therefore, a shattering defeat for socialism. It illustrated, perhaps, the victory of common sense and practicality which has rescued France from more than one crisis,

for it was clear enough that a country on the brink of economic disaster was hardly the place for utopian experiments. The government had urgently to find money, yet with the future so uncertain the policy of raising loans by the issue of government bonds was a miserable failure. Appeals to French patriotism were in vain, yet, equally, to increase the level of taxation was unthinkable. There remained the possibility of reducing government spending.

For this reason, if for no other, Louis Blan's idea of co-operative production was doomed. He and other Socialists had advocated the setting-up of National Workshops, where workers would both own and control the processes of production and would divide the profits among themselves. Initially, the state would provide the capital to buy premises, machines and materials, but thereafter workers would be free to run their own affairs independently of their former capitalist masters. Part of the profits would be set aside to purchase more workshops, so that ultimately the whole of the nation's economy would be socialist.

Obviously, such ideas held great attraction for the poor and unemployed of the French cities, but equally clearly they faced immense problems of finance and organisation. It was, to say the least, unlikely that the middle classes who had sunk their fortunes in industry would voluntarily renounce their ownership, and the new minister of public works, who himself opposed the whole idea, was easily able to wreck any chance of success that the National Workshops might have had. Although work of a kind was certainly provided for the unemployed, he made no attempt to select men for tasks according to their skill, and no attempt to create work which could show a profit. Men were directed into planting trees or digging trenches which they then filled in again. Workers soon became disheartened, abandoned their support of the Socialists and spent their time either in idleness or fruitless political agitation. The National Workshops had skilfully been turned into objects of public ridicule and scorn.

Above left: A charge by the Municipal Guard on 22 February 1848.
Left: street fighting in Paris.
(Bibliothèque Nationale, Paris.)
Above: A painting by Delacroix, Liberty Leading the People. *(Musée du Louvre, Paris.)*

The days of June

Meanwhile, reaction was setting in in the government. All real power was concentrated in an Executive Committee of five members which, although it contained Republicans like Lamartine and Arago, had no Socialist representative. In May an armed demonstration resulted in the arrest of the Socialist leaders Barbès, Blanqui and Albert, and the closure of the revolutionary clubs, while one of the first acts of the newly-elected Assembly was to order the shutting of the National Workshops. Workers were given the choice of two unattractive alternatives—military service in Algeria or work draining the mosquito-infested swamps of Sologne in central France. For the middle classes, it seemed a good way of removing a disorderly mob from Paris, but the men of the National Workshops who had once dreamed of being their own masters, had no intention of accepting either. Once more the barricades went up in the streets of Paris, but this time with Republican against Socialist.

For a while it seemed that the government forces were taking little action. In fact, General Cavaignac was first cutting off the infected areas of the city like the Latin Quarter, and then making organised attacks, but only after several days of very bitter fighting did these become successful. Middle class opinion had been outraged by accounts of the brutality of the rebels such as the fatal injury of the Archbishop of Paris who had tried to intervene in the dispute, and the Assembly now wreaked terrible vengeance; 10,000 Socialists were executed, a further 15,000 imprisoned. In future the Socialist working class and the Republican middle class, who had once fought together behind the barricades, were divided by the blood spilt in June 1848. The inevitability of the class war, which Karl Marx had predicted, seemed to be amply justified by the turn of French events.

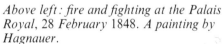

Above left: fire and fighting at the Palais Royal, 28 February 1848. A painting by Hagnauer.
Above: a portrait painted in 1838 by M. L. Mongez of Ledru-Rollin, a leading member of the provisional government in 1848. (Musée Carnavalet, Paris.)
Left: members of the provisional government—Arago, Garnier-Pagès, Marie, Ledru-Rollin and Lamartine. (Bibliothèque Nationale, Paris.)

The return of Louis Bonaparte

With public order re-established so dearly, the first task of the Assembly was to prepare a constitution. That this was to be a Republican one was never in doubt, but beyond this there were almost as many opinions as deputies. Ultimately, a constitution resembling, in some respects, that of the United States of America was agreed, its main principle being to have a president with executive power sufficient to guarantee public order. He was to be chosen by universal suffrage for a period of four years—long enough, it was hoped, to make his mark, but not to establish a dynasty. As the legislative arm there would be a single National Assembly, also elected by universal suffrage, though the precise relationship between the Assembly and the president was not clearly defined. The principle of

111

'the right to work' was specifically not mentioned: it was replaced by 'the freedom to work'.

The presidential elections took place in December. A number of candidates entered the lists—Lamartine, the revered writer and Republican, Cavaignac, the general who had saved Paris from the mob, two Socialist leaders and, finally, Louis Bonaparte, returned from England where he had quietly been waiting for the call. He was elected at the head of the poll by a majority of more than four million votes.

He was the son of Napoleon's brother, Louis, who had for some years under the empire held the throne of Holland. By a series of unlikely chances—the early death of Napoleon's own son, then that of his elder brother, killed during *Carbonari* violence in Italy—he had become the heir to the Bonapartist succession and legend. Although possessing few of his uncle's qualities, Louis had lived a life of some daring and adventure in Switzerland and Italy, had twice before made a bid for French power, and had escaped from his final imprisonment in the fortress of Ham, to England in 1846. Here he waited until the events of February 1848 brought him rushing back to France. At forty he was still hesitant and timid, a poor orator who fumbled his speech as a newly-elected deputy, but he had the name of Napoleon which still passed in every Frenchman's memory for discipline, power and military renown.

The Conservative Republic

There could be no mistaking the relief with which the French electors turned to a candidate who had the advantage not only of name but of having been apart from the vacillations and shabbiness of French politics in recent years. Here, it was thought, was a president who would be above politics, who could be loved at home and respected abroad. Louis was elected overwhelmingly, polling 5,400,000 votes compared with 1,400,000 for Cavaignac: the rest were far behind, at the very bottom the poet Lamartine with a mere 20,000.

Elections for the Legislative Assembly were held a year later—in May 1849. The result was a major defeat for the moderate Republicans and a victory for the Conservatives, but also significant was a substantial gain for the extreme Republicans led by Ledru-Rollin. The strange situation was already occurring that out of a republican

revolution had emerged a president who was a prince, and an Assembly elected by universal suffrage which was solidly conservative and, indeed, contained many royalists. One of the first acts of the new government was to send a French expeditionary force to Rome, not to support the republic of Mazzini, but to overthrow it. Ledru-Rollin and others who had attempted an insurrection against the campaign were sent into exile.

It soon became clear that the Republic and its president were no democrats or tolerators of free thought. The spread of socialism, it was believed, had originated with teachers of 'advanced' ideas in schools and colleges, and in order to prevent such people from practising, the Falloux Law of 1850 was passed, limiting the right to teach to those only who held a university degree. An even greater restriction followed in May 1850, when the parliamentary franchise was made conditional on having lived in the constituency for three years and having never had any court conviction, even for the most trivial offence. This removed the franchise from 3,000,000 of the former 9,000,000 voters: in particular, it hit at Socialists and extreme Republicans, many of whom had been technically guilty of political offences, and were precisely the people who never stayed long in the same place. The Assembly had very effectively removed political power from their opponents without incurring the unpopularity of having restricted the franchise by a property qualification.

Louis Napoleon was sufficiently astute to let it be known that he personally disapproved of the measure, and thus could continue to stand as the representative of freedom and equality. It seems likely that he was already preparing the ground for his *coup d'état*, the seizure of power by which he could again make Bonapartism a reality. In retrospect, there is an inevitability about the course of events.

The elected president found himself in a chamber in which he had no personal following and from which he could expect no support: he was, by temperament, a liberal and a nationalist, yet he was forced to acquiesce in conservative policies at home, even to support the pope against the Republicans in Italy. The constitution stipulated that the president should hold office for four years, and was not re-eligible. The nephew of Napoleon, who had risked all to return to France, was unlikely to accept such transitory power.

Napoleon's coup d'état *of December 1851,*
was treated with indifference by the majority
of the French people. A few republican
deputies like Baudin tried unsuccessfully to
persuade the workers to resist.
Above: the death of the Republic. A satirical
drawing entitled 'Burial of a young person
after ten months of suffering—her friends
inconsolable at her loss'. (Bibliothèque
Nationale, Paris.)
Above right: Louis Napoleon, the prince
president, returns to Paris after a
triumphant tour of the provinces in 1852.
(Musée de Versailles.)
Right: Baudin dies bravely, but
unsupported, at the barricade of Saint-
Antoine, a suburb of Paris, 3 December
1851. A painting by Ernest Pichio.
(Musée Carnavalet, Paris.)

The *coup d'état* of December 1851

The president now carefully prepared the ground. First, the military governor of Paris was dismissed on a pretext, and replaced by one of his own supporters. The Africa Corps, on whose loyalty he could depend, were also quartered in the capital. He next undertook a series of tours throughout the provinces, rallying support at mass meetings in which his supporters had been carefully planted to lead the cry of '*Vive l'Empereur*'. Finally, he began a campaign to alter Article 45 of the constitution to allow the president to serve for a further term of office of four years. In doing so, Louis Bonaparte probably calculated on the Assembly's rejection, and, if so, his prediction was justified. His amendment to the constitution was finally rejected in July 1851.

From this time, an open conflict had really become inevitable, but the president still chose his time carefully. The selected date was to be 2 December, the anniversary of his uncle's coronation as Emperor of France and of his great military victory of Austerlitz. On the evening of the 1st, he gave a splendid reception at the Elysée Palace, where he was seen to be unusually charming and courteous. At one point, however, he slipped away to give instructions to an inner circle of conspirators—his half-brother Morny, Maupas the Prefect of Police, and Saint-Armand the military commander. During the night the plan was put into effect —occupation of the Assembly, arrest of all the principal leaders who might have organised resistance, including Thiers and Cavaignac, and military occupation of strategic points in Paris. An announcement was made dissolving the Chamber of Deputies and re-introducing universal suffrage.

When Paris awoke the next morning, the takeover was already accomplished. A few deputies tried to resist, objecting that the president had broken his oath, had violated the constitution, and was therefore deposed. Few took any notice, and those like Victor Hugo who tried to urge the people to take up arms against a tyrant found no support. Parisians had suffered and died at the barricades only three years before, and had gained nothing from their middle class allies. Louis Napoleon was seen as a democratic deliverer who would restore the Rights of Man and again make France respected throughout the courts of Europe.

The *coup d'état* succeeded brilliantly in a city overcome by lethargy and bored by the succession of civil disorders. One of the few instances of courage occurred when the deputy Baudin was urging the workers to help him build a barricade, and one of them called out: 'Do you think we are going to get ourselves killed to protect your twenty-five francs a day?' (The official salary of a deputy). Baudin replied: 'Stay there, my friend, and you will see someone killed for twenty-five francs a day.' Shortly afterwards he was killed at the barricade. On 4 December there was shooting on the

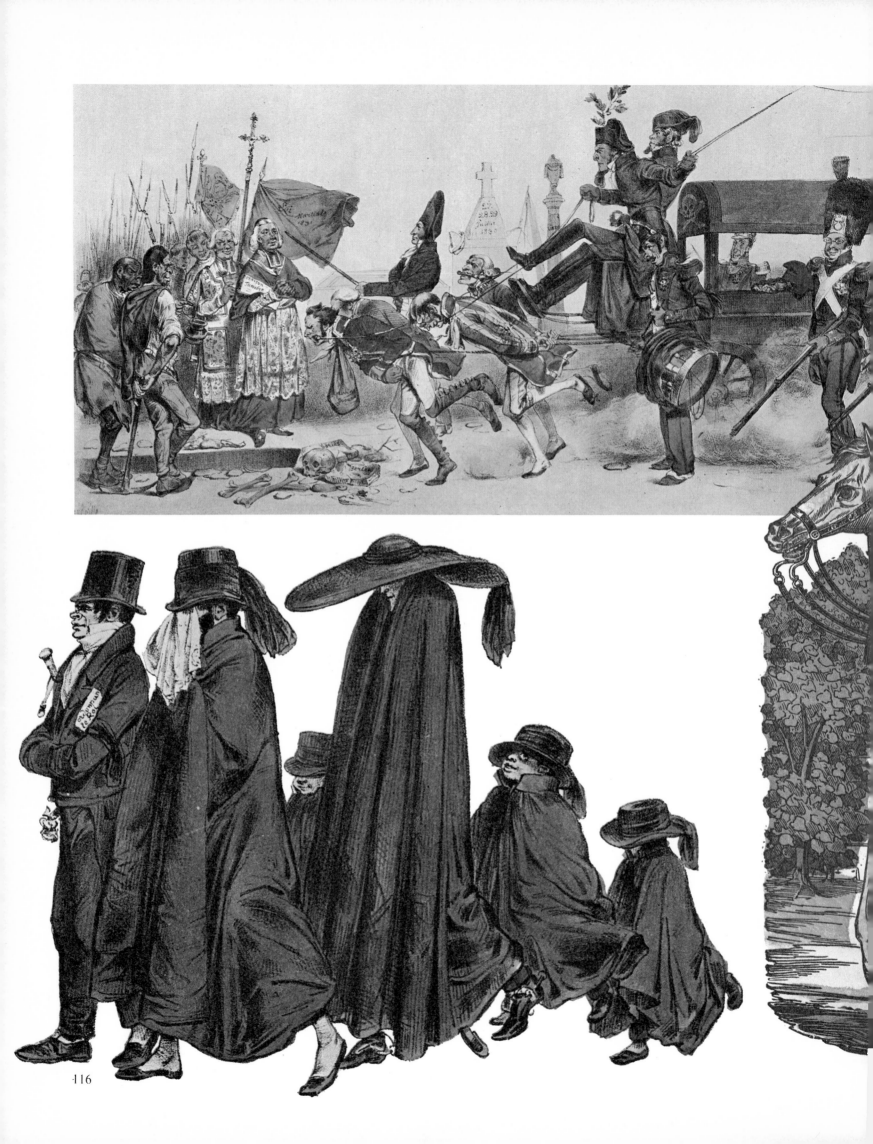

boulevards which terrorised Parisians, and armed risings in the provinces which were put down with terrible severity. In all, some 1,200 innocent citizens were killed in the coup, 10,000 more deported, and sixty deputies, including Victor Hugo, expelled from France. Louis Napoleon's seizure of power was thus achieved by fraud, duress and murder, yet it also had the overwhelming backing of the French people. On 21 December a national plebiscite was held, and by 7,350,000 votes to a mere 650,000 France expressed her approval of the prince-president's acts.

'The empire is peace'

A new constitution became immediately necessary and was quickly drawn up. The President of the Republic was to hold office for ten years. Under him was to be a Council of State, a silent body whose debates were never made public, but which had the crucial role of proposing legislation to the Legislative Assembly. There was also to be a Senate of dignitaries and notables. The new constitution thus approached that of a monarchy. giving considerably greater power and security to the president than would be usual under a republic.

Clearly, Louis' position was now firmly established, but would the European powers accept a Bonapartist on what had, for all practical purposes, become the 'throne' of France?

Louis Napoleon, elated with his success, had already observed to the Sardinian Prime Minister, 'Now I can do what I want, I shall do something for Italy', and it was the fear that a revived Bonapartism in Europe might reawaken nationalist feelings among subject Italians, Poles, Hungarians and Slavs that most alarmed the rulers of Austria and Russia. Even in Britain, where there was admiration for the president's liberal and democratic ideas, there was also concern that a Bonaparte was again in command in France, placed there by the force of arms and known to be looking for military glory. His frequently asserted claim that 'the Empire is Peace' seemed genuine enough, however. Britain recognised the new president, Russia and Austria remained suspicious but had no way of intervening in the situation.

Precisely a year after the seizure of power, on 2 December 1852, a hereditary Empire replaced the Republic which had had nothing republican about it except the name. In a strange calm a new empire was born and a new figure stepped onto the European stage. Still not acceptable socially, the new emperor was not permitted to marry into any of the legitimate royal families of Europe, but in January 1853 took as wife a beautiful young Spanish countess, Eugénie of Montijo.

Left: the marriage of Napoleon III to the
Spanish Countess Eugénie of Montijo,
January 1853. (Bibliothèque Nationale,
Paris.)
Above: the emperor receives the Siamese
Ambassadors at Fontainebleau, June 1861
(Musée de Versailles.)
Right: Baron Haussmann, who planned the
great rebuilding of Paris. Though brilliantly
conceived, his schemes became a byword
for extravagance and financial scandals.
(Musée Carnavalet, Paris.)

The aristocratic empire

For the first few years of his reign the emperor ruled personally and with a strong hand. Normal political life practically ceased: the opposition was either cowed or exiled, and the few who, like Victor Hugo, dared to raise their voice against 'the Little Napoleon' made no headway.

The press was effectively muzzled, and any criticism of the emperor quickly resulted in suppression. Even elections, which had been the great national pre-occupation of recent years, ceased to be of much interest when only loyal candidates were able to stand. The local prefects kept a complete control over the conduct of election campaigns, to such good effect that when opposition candidates tried to present themselves they found it impossible to hire halls for meetings or to find printers who would publish their literature. Prefects openly canvassed for the 'official' candidates, factory owners warned their workers to 'vote

properly'. Political passion had, for the time being, been suffocated.

In some respects the France of the early empire seemed to turn back to the attitudes and values of Louis Philippe. If political life was sterile and unrewarding, at least in the new stability of domestic conditions one might make money and enjoy oneself. It was an era of heavy investment and great banking development, the government leading the way by financing enormous public works, road and railway building programmes. Paris itself was to be reconstructed, the Prefect of the Seine, Baron Haussmann, being commissioned to prepare plans to build the most magnificent capital in Europe, a city to dazzle the foreigners who had scorned the elected emperor.

Parisian life

Great new boulevards were cut through the heart of Paris, at once giving a plan and symmetry to the capital which it had never

had before and, in the process, destroying many of the slums which had disfigured it. The wide roads with their tarmac surfaces were beautiful and impressive: at the same time, they made army manoeuvres easier, and deprived Parisians of the paving-stones which rebellious mobs had been accustomed to fling from behind the barricades. Haussmann's remodelling of Paris therefore had many motives—economic, social aesthetic and military. Not least important, it provided employment for those evicted from the National Workshops, and gave immense opportunities to investors, speculators and businessmen of many kinds.

Paris in the 1850's was a city of feverish activity and frivolous gaiety, reflected admirably in the popular light operas of

Offenbach, *The Tales of Hoffmann* and *La Belle Hélène*. The reputation of Paris as a city of easy virtue, if not positive wickedness, dates especially from this period, when the emperor of the French could devote time to playing Blind Man's Buff or, less innocently, to his mistresses.

For many of the working class, too, times were good, with regular employment, trade booming and rising wages. For that growing section who now had some margin of income over necessary expenditure there were new pleasures, new recreations, great new stores like 'Bon Marché' where customers could find all that they needed, at moderate prices, under one roof, or could simply come to stare.

But the countryside also shared in the

prosperity of the capital. Roads and railways brought a new mobility to people and goods, enabling farm produce to be sold profitably in the growing towns, and bringing the benefits of civilisation to formerly remote areas. Agriculture was still the mainstay of the French economy, some two-thirds of the whole population still living on the land and cultivating their small peasant farms. For them, the political events of the last few years had been remote, almost irrelevant, but now they could take pride in a revived empire and share in the benefits of a programme of national development. Even the sandy wastes of the Landes area in western France came to be planted with fir-trees to provide pit props for the expanding coal-mines, while in the Alps the daring project

was begun of driving a tunnel through the heart of Mont Cenis.

But for the Second Empire to become a complete reality it needed to spread its wings beyond the confines of France and establish a colonial hegemony. It was in pursuance of such an object and in the face of ridicule and scepticism by Britain, that in 1859 work was begun on cutting the Suez Canal in Egypt. A sea route to India and the East could bring back the Mediterranean into importance in world trade, could revive the great ports of southern France and begin to move back the balance of maritime power from the British-dominated Atlantic. With these great purposes in view the foreign policy of the empire was bent towards extending French influence throughout the Mediterranean

world—intervention in Italian affairs, the pacification of Algeria and the defence of the Holy Places in Palestine which was to involve her in a victorious war against the despotic power of Russia. With the signing of the Treaty of Paris in 1856. France had successfully reasserted her place in the conduct of European affairs.

The Orsini affair

For the first few years the reign of the new emperor was undisturbed by the political crises which had come to be regarded as almost the normal condition of French life. The opposition party made some small gains in the elections of 1857, though insufficient to constitute any real threat to the security of

121

the government which was bringing an unaccustomed measure of order and prosperity to the country. In 1858, however, a more serious event occurred. As a young *carbonari* before his accession to power Louis Napoleon vowed that he would help the Italians to liberate their country from the Austrians: now, as emperor, he was more prudent and cautious, seeming to betray his Italian friends. One of the most extreme of the Italian nationalists, Orsini, was driven to make an attempt on the emperor's life, his bombs killing or wounding over a hundred people. Napoleon himself escaped injury.

The 'Orsini Affair' was, however, influential in shaping French attitudes. At home, the attempt provided the government with good grounds for tightening security by permitting the prefects to deport any suspect by simple administrative order. Over 300 Frenchmen were so exiled on evidence which would scarcely have satisfied a court of law. France quietly acquiesced in a policy which some regarded as a move towards autocracy,

even dictatorship, on the part of an all-powerful emperor.

The liberal empire

Unaccountably, however, Napoleon suddenly retracted his policy and proceeded to introduce a series of liberal reforms. In fact, it seems likely that it was the growing opposition from Catholics and industrialists, who had formerly supported the regime, that forced the change, Napoleon having increasingly to seek an alliance with the political left as the right deserted him.

The Catholics he had offended by not sufficiently backing the temporal power of the Pope in Italy. Industrialists were claiming that the Free Trade Treaty signed with Britain in 1860, which would allow the passage of goods without duty between the two countries, would ruin the French economy. Napoleon, ahead of his people, had become a confirmed free trader, impressed by the success of the policy in

122

England, but most French industrialists believed that their continued prosperity depended on maintaining the protection afforded by the tariff system, which their goods enjoyed in the home market. Now the two disparate groups made common cause in resentment against the dictatorial aspects of the regime which they had once been only too ready to support.

The Catholics were the first to launch an open attack against the emperor in the columns of the influential Catholic newspaper *L'Univers*. The government responded by suppressing the religious society of Saint Vincent de Paul. But the chief power of the Church lay in its control over the schools, and the Minister of Education now decided to attack this. His real desire—to establish a system of state elementary schools throughout the land—proved impracticable but he did set up the lycèes (secondary schools) for girls in direct competition with the convents, and himself planned a course of ethics and morals to replace instruction in religion.

The great struggle between church and state —a central issue in European politics since the Middle Ages—had been reopened.

The emperor therefore had to fall back on his old enemies, the liberal Republicans, and in order to gain their support concessions were required. An amnesty was granted for many political offenders, freedom of speech was allowed to deputies and the right of publication of parliamentary debates. In the general election of 1863 the opposition polled two million votes, and Thiers, the liberal, was returned to office. It was also part of the new policy to make a greater appeal to the working classes, and with this in view trade unions were granted the legal right to strike in 1864. Two years previously, permission had been granted for a delegation of working men to go to London to meet English workers: out of this meeting was born in 1864 the International Working Men's Association which, under the influence of Karl Marx, was to become a powerful force in international socialism.

The parliamentary empire

Once again, the pattern of events which had shaped French history ever since the revolution of 1789 reasserted itself. Autocracy could survive so long as the people were content: when opposition appeared, concessions had to be made which only served to demonstrate how little freedom the people really had, and whetted the appetite for more.

In other ways, too, the strength of the regime was ebbing. The strong men of 1848, including the emperor himself, were now older and feebler than they had been twenty years before. Foreign affairs had not gone with the flair and success that an empire seemed to demand, and, in particular, France had been obliged to watch with growing concern the rise to power of Prussia and her overwhelming defeat of Austria on the battlefields of Sadowa in 1866. The policy of concession in no way abated the mounting opposition to the

The plebiscite of 1870 only concealed the real weakness of the empire. Growing discontent among workers found expression in strikes and demonstrations such as this by women outside the great Creusot steel works in April 1870. (Bibliothèque Nationale, Paris.)

regime, which became increasingly dangerous as Republicans and Socialists sank their former differences and became reconciled in a common opposition to the policies of the Empire. The failing power of the government was amply demonstrated in the elections of 1867 when, despite all efforts to gain support, its majority was drastically reduced, and the combined opposition of Catholics, Republicans and Socialists polled more than 3,000,000 votes. Further concessions to freedom of the press and of assembly followed in a desperate attempt to curry favour.

For the last two years of his reign the emperor was the subject of ridicule, even public dislike. One of the consequences of the now free press was an outpouring of satirical comment on Napoleon and his government, most brilliantly handled by the journalist Rochefort in *La Lanterne*. By 1869, when in fresh general elections the opposition polled almost half the total votes of France, the situation had deteriorated to one of extreme danger where either the Empire must make some drastic bid for popularity or must quickly fall.

At this critical point in French affairs, help suddenly came from an unexpected quarter. One of the Republican opposition to be elected was Emile Ollivier, at first a bitter critic of the emperor but whose ideas gradually changed to support. By 1869 he found

himself prime minister. His responsibility, as he saw it, was to the Assembly rather than to the emperor, and here he gradually built up a powerful group of moderate liberals which became known as 'the Third Party'.

By 1870 it seemed that a parliamentary Empire modelled on the lines of the British political system, might at last become a reality. A new constitution was framed on liberal principles, submitted to a national plebiscite, and accepted, to the immense relief of the emperor, by nearly, 6,000,000 votes. The Republican-Socialist opposition was crushed, and the Empire seemed even more secure, and rooted in popular support, than it had been in 1852. 'On whichever side we look,' declared the new prime minister, 'there is an absence of troublesome questions; at no moment has the maintenance of peace in Europe been better secured.' Precisely one month later a war broke out which was to sweep away Ollivier, Louis Napoleon and the Empire, and to result in the appearance of a powerful, united Germany on the stage of Europe.

REACTION AND LIBERALISM (1815-48); THE DECLINE OF TURKEY

	Austrian Empire	Revolution and nationalism	Ottoman Empire
1815		Second Treaty of Paris (1815)	
		Napoleon banished	
		Holy Roman Empire reconstituted as German Confederation (1815)	
		The Holy Alliance	
		Congress of Aix-la-Chapelle	
	Carlsbad Decrees—highest point of Austrian influence in Germany (1819)	Peterloo Massacre, Manchester (1819)	
1820		Liberal revolt in Naples (1820)	
		Constitution of 1812 (Liberal) proclaimed in Spain. Abolition of Inquisition (1820)	Revolt of Ali Pasha against Turks (1820)
			Greek War of Independence (1821)
	Francis I recognises old Hungarian constitution (1825)	Civil War in northern Spain	
		Portugal recognises Brazilian independence	Turkish fleet destroyed at Navarino (1827)
		First of many peasant revolts in Russia	Turks evacuate Greece
		Belgian independence recognised by Holy Alliance	Treaty of Adrianople: Russia abandons European conquests
1830		July Revolution in Paris (1830	
	Austria recognises Greek independence (1831)	Revolts in Modena, Parma, Bologna, Romagna	
		Poland becomes Russian province (1831)	
	Metternich suppresses liberal risings in Saxony, Bavaria, Brunswick, Hesse-Cassel	Parliamentary Reform Act in England (1832)	Mehemet Ali invades Syria (1832)
		Carlist war in Spain	Treaty of Unkiar-Skelessi (1833)
		Democratic local government introduced in Norway	Revolt of Syrians against Ibrahim (1834)
	Austria supports Anglo-Russian accord over Turkey (1839)	Irish Poor Law Act	Battle of Nesib: Ibrahim defeats Turks (1839)
1840		Marriage of Queen Victoria and Prince Albert of Saxe-Coburg (1840)	
		Repeal Association founded in Ireland	Peace between Sultan and Mehemet Ali (1841)
	Annexation of Cracow (1846)	Trial of O'Connell in Ireland	
		Irish potato disease spreads to continent	
	Accession of Francis Joseph (1848)	Revolution in Paris: Second Republic (1848)	
		Federal constitution approved in Switzerland Revolutions in Berlin, Vienna, Prague, Budapest, Rome, Venice, Milan, Naples (1848)	
	Hungarian Republic proclaimed (1849)		
1850		Factory Act passed in England	

Further Reading List

Britain

G. Kitson Clark, *The Making of Victorian England* (London, 1965)

E. L. Woodward, *The Age of Reform 1815–1870 (The Oxford History of England)* (London, 1962)

A. Aspinall (ed.), *English Historical Documents 1815–1870* (London, 1967)

T. S. Ashton, *The Industrial Revolution, 1760–1830* (London, 1969)

E. J. Hobsbaum, *Industry and Empire: An Economic History of Britain since 1750* (London, 1968)

J. L. and Barbara Hammond, *The Age of the Chartists 1832–54: A Study of Discontent* (London, 1967)

E. Halévy, *A History of the English People in the Nineteenth Century*, 6 vols (London, 1961)

C. Woodham-Smith, *The Reason Why* (London, 1953)

Europe

Harold Nicolson, *The Congress of Vienna* (London, 1961)

A. J. P. Taylor, *The Course of German History* (London, 1962)

L. C. B. Seaman, *From Vienna to Versailles* (London, 1955)

A. J. Whyte, *The Evolution of Modern Italy, 1710–1920* (London, 1944)

G. M. Trevelyan, *Garibaldi and the Making of Italy* (London, 1948)

J. L. Talmon, *Romanticism and Revolt, Europe 1815–1848* (London, 1967)

W. O. Henderson, *The Industrialisation of Europe, 1780–1914* (London, 1969)

Russia

Hugh Seton-Watson, *The Decline of Imperial Russia* (London, 1964)

Bernard Pares, *A History of Russia* (London, 1955)

B. H. Sumner, *A Survey of Russian History*, second ed. (London, 1948)

Acknowledgments

10–11, 11, 12–13, 16–17, 17, 18–19, 20 Above and below, 21, 22 Above and below, 24, 30, 32, 33 Above, 43, 44, 46, 47, 48, 48–9, 49, 50–1, 51, 52, 53, 54, 54–5, 55, 56, 58, 58–9, 59, 62–3, 74, 75, 76, 77, 78, 78–9 Above and below, 80, 81, 82 Above and below, 83, 84–5, 85, 86, 86–7, 88, 89, 90, 91, 92 Josse; 95 Centre, Jacky Requet, 98 Below, Jacky Requet; 100 Above, Josse; 101 Above, Jacky Requet. Below, Muller; 102 Above and below, 102–3, Josse; 106–7 Jacky Requet; 109 Josse; 110 Above, Jacky Requet, 111 Jacky Requet; 114 Below, 114–15, 118–19, 119, 120–1 Josse; 121 Below, Jacky Requet.

Index

REFERENCES TO CAPTIONS ARE
IN ITALICS

Abdul Medjid, sultan 71, 73
Abel, Niels 23
Abestuzhev *81*
Act of Union (1800) 33
Adrianople, Treaty of (1829) 69
Africa Corps 115
Aix-la-Chapelle, congress in (1818) 45
Albert (Alexandre Martin) 106, 111
Albert of Saxe-Coburg, Prince *33*, 35
Alexander I, Tsar 50, 66, 75, 81; death
  of (1825) 76
Alexander II, Tsar 70, 74, 75, 87;
  assassination 89; reforms 82–84, 86,
  90
Alexandra Feodorovna, Tsarina *77*
Ali Pasha (Turkish foreign minister) 73
Ali Pasha of Janina *61*, 65
Alma, battle of the 73
American War of Independence
  (1776–83) 39
Ampère, André 23
Ancien régime 19, 93, 95, 97, 98
Anglican Church 26
Anti-Corn Law League 39
Arago, Dominique *19*, 23, 111
Arakcheyev, Alexei 75
Arkwright, Sir Richard 11, 27
Artois, Count of 94
Aspern, battle of (1809) *49*
Augustus, prince of Prussia *48*
Austerlitz, battle of 115
Austria,
  at war with Hungary 59–61;
  revolution in 57–9

Balaklava, battle of *67*, 73–4
Balbo, Cesare 50, 54
Bank of England 26
Barbès, Armand 104, 111
Barings (banking house) 17
Baudin, Jean Baptiste *114*, 115
Bazard, Saint-Amand 21
Berlin 58
Berry, Duchess of *93*, 103
Berry, Duke of 94; assassination 97
Biot, Jean Baptiste 23
Bismarck, Prince Otto von 6, 63
Blanc, Louis 2, 105, 106, 109
Blanqui, Louis 104, 111
Blücher, Marshal 25
Boers 40
Bonapartistism 100, 104, 117
Bordeaux, Duke of 99
Boris Godunov (Pushkin) 81
Bosnia, revolts in 72
Bourbons, restoration of 93–4, *95*
'Bourgeois revolution' (1830) 79, 98–9,
  103
Britain. *see* England
Büchner, Georg 50
Burschenschaft (student body) 45, 50
Byron, Lord 24, 66, 81; death 25

Cadiz, revolution in (1820) 45–8, 49
Calomarde, Francisco (Spanish minister
  of justice) 49
Canaris, Constantin *62, 63*, 67
Canning, George 49, 66
Capitalism 12, *16*
Carboneria 48, 50; exiled in Paris 49
Carlsbad, congress of 45
Carlyle, Thomas 35
Carnot, Sadi 23
Caroline of Brunswick 30–2
Carrel, Nicolas 100
Castle of Heidelberg (Wallis) *20*
Castlereagh, Viscount 49
Catherine II of Russia 75, 76
Catholic Church 32–3, 72–3, 97, 100,
  123, 124
Cavour, Count 50, 54, 59, 63, 74
Chamber of Deputies (French) 94, 98,
  102, 105
Cavaignac, General 111, 112, 115
Chadwick, Edwin 34
Chambord, Count of 93
Champollion, Jean François 24
Charbonneries 96, 122
Charles, archduke of Austria *49*
Charles X, king of France 66, 97–8, 99,

100, 103
Charles Albert of Piedmont 54, 58
Charles Felix, King 49
Chartism 38, 39, 42
Chateaubriand, François de 24, 94
Chatham, Earl of 25
Chernyshevsky, Nikolai 87
Chevalier, Michel 15
Chevreul, Michel 23
Children, employment of in England 18,
  36
Christians in Turkey 63–4
Civil War, American 42; English 32
Cobbett, William 27
Cobden, Richard 39
Coleridge, Samuel Taylor 24
Commonwealth, origins of 41–2
Communist League *19*, 22
Communist Manifesto (published 1848)
  22, 106
Congrégation (French) 97
Conservative Party (in England) 17, 32,
  39
Conservatives (in France) 112
Constant; Benjamin 94, 97
Constantine, Grand Duke 50, 76, 77, 79
'Constitutionists' (in France) 94, 98; in
  power 95–6
Corn Laws (1815) 32; repeal of (1846)
  15, 17, 32, 38
Cort, Henry 11
Cortes 45
Courrier Français 94
Cousin, Victor 97
Crimean War *67, 70*, 73–4, 75;
  consequences of 82
Custozza, battle of (1848) 58
Cuvier, Georges 23, 24

Dalton, John 23
Darwin, Charles 24
Das Kapital (Marx) 17
Daumier, Honoré 103
Dead Souls (Gogol) 8
Deák, Ferenc 57
Decazes, Elie (French prime minister)
  96, 97
Decembrists 76–7, *77*, 81
De Custine, Marquis 78
Delacroix, Eugène, *109*
De Lesseps, Ferdinand 74
Delhi, battle for (1857) *38*
De Musset, Alfred *22*
De Tocqueville, Alexis 52, 78, 105
De Vigny, Alfred 24
Diet of Frankfurt (1832) 50
Diet of Prague 57
Disraeli, Benjamin 35, 38, 39
Dostoevsky, Feodor 81, 82, 87
Duma (Russian municipal council) 86

Eastern Question 59, *61*, 63–4, 71, 72
East India Company 35, 40
Edward, duke of Kent *30*, 35
Egypt, army 66–9, 72; conflict with
  Europe 71–2; economic development
  68; war with Turkey 70–1
Electricity, development of 23
Electromagnetism, laws of 23
Encyclopaedia Britannica 90
Enfantin, Barthélemy 21
Engels, Friedrich 22, 86, 106
England, after Waterloo 25; civil
  service 35; class war 42; depression
  (1848) 38; free trade 12, 15, 35, 38–9;
  industrialisation 11–12, 27; industrial
  revolution 11, 25, *29*; influence on
  Turkey 70–1, 73; parliamentary
  aristocracy 25–6; postwar depression
  27–30, 32; railways 15; Romantic age
  24–5
Eugene Onegin (Pushkin) 81
Europe, agriculture in 10–11, 18;
  industrial development 11–15; new
  social structure 17; peace treaties
  (1815) 43–4

Fabvier, Baron Charles *61*, 66
Factory Act (1833) 36, 38
Falloux Law (1850) 112, *120*
Faraday, Michael *19*, 23
Far East 39–40
Fathers and Sons (Turgenev) 81
Federation of Just Men. *see* Communist
  League
Ferdinand, emperor of Austria 59
Ferdinand I of Naples 48, 59
Ferdinand VII, king of Spain 45, 49

First World War 74, 90
Fourier, François 21, 106
Foy, General 97
France, anti-republican feeling in 95;
  constitution of 1815 94; development
  of railways *14*, 15; education 123;
  industrialisation 12, 123; invasion of
  Russia (1812) 75; July Monarchy 99;
  political crisis in (1829) 98; revolt of
  the silk workers 100–4; revolution of
  1830 79, 98–9, 103; revolution of
  1848 105, *107*
Francis I, king *49*
Francis Joseph, archduke 59, 61;
  emperor *74*
Frankfurt Parliament 58–61
Frederick, emperor of Austria *48*, 57
Frederick William III, king of Prussia
  49, 77
Frederick William IV, king of Prussia
  53, 58, 61
Frederick William of Prussia, Prince *33*
Freemasonry 76
Free Trade (in Britain) 12, 15, 35, 38–9,
  41, 50, 122
French Revolution 43, 44, 52, 54, 64, 76,
  79, 93, 98–9, 103, 105, *107*
Fuseli, Henri 24

Galvani, Luigi 23
Garibaldi, Giuseppe 58, 59
Garnier-Pagès, Etienne 100, *111*
Gauss, Karl 22
Gay-Lussac, Joseph *19*, 23
Gazette de France 94
George III, king of England 25, *29*, 30,
  35
George IV, king of England 33, 35
Germany, industrialisation 11–12;
  reforms 50; revolutions of 1848–9 *56*,
  58, 59–62
Gioberti, Abbé 50
Gladstone, William Ewart 36, 39
Glorious Revolution (1688) 25
Goethe, Johann Wolfgang von *20*, 24
Gogol, Nikolai 81
Grand National Consolidated Trade
  Union (1833–4) 21, 36
Great Exhibition (1851) 42
Great Trek (1833) 40
Greece, independence 64–6, 69; receives
  help from Europe 66; rising (1821)
  64–6; war with Turkish Empire 66
Greek Orthodox Church 64, 72–4
Grey, Lord 34
Guizot, François 94, 97–8, 100, 103–5,
  109

Habsburg Empire 58
Hackert, Carl Ludwig *20*
Haidouks (Serbian guerrillas) 64
Hargreaves, James 11
Haussman Baron *118*, 119–20
Hegel, Friedrich 86
Heine, Heinrich 50
Hellenic Constitution 67
Henry, Prince (heir of Charles X) 103
Hero of our Time (Lermontov) 81
Herzen, Alexander 81, 83
Hetairie (Greek secret society) 65
Holy Alliance 24, 43–4, 49, 69, 75–6
Holy places, dispute over 72–3
Homer 24
Hopes (banking house) 17
House of Commons 17, 26
House of Lords 25, *29*, 34
Hugo, Victor 24, 115, 117, 119
'Hundred Days, The' 95, 104
Hungary 59–61; at war with Austria
  59–61; revolution in 58
Hunt, Henry 27, 30
Huskisson, William 15, 32

Ibrahim (son of Mehemet Ali) 70, 71
Imam Schamyl 89
'Independents' (French political group)
  94
India 37, 39–40
Industrialisation in Europe 11–18, 32,
  40, 42, 52
Inkerman, battle of *67*
Intelligentsia in Russia 81–2
International Exhibition (Paris 1867) 42
International Working Men's
  Association 123
Irish Famine 39, 54
Irish Home Rule *29*
Italy 57–8

Jellachich, Count Joseph, Croatian
  governor 59
Jesuits in France 97
Joule, James 23
July Monarchy 99–100, 103

Kara George 64
Karakozov 89
Keats, John 24
Kollár, Jan 57
Kolokol ('The Bell', Herzen) 83
Kossuth, Louis 57, 58, 59, *61*
Kotzebue, August, assassination of
  (1819) *44*, 45
Koutaieh, Treaty of (1833) 70
Krüdener, Julie de 75
Krupp 12
Kugelen, Gerhard von *22*

Lacordaire, Jean Baptiste 19
Lafayette, Marquis de 94, 97, 99, 100
Laffitte, Jacques 100, 103
Laibach, congress of (1821) 48–9, 66
La Lanterne 124
Lallemant, Pierre 13
Lamarck, Jean Baptiste 24
Lamartine, Alphonse de 24, 105, 106,
  111, 112
Lamennais, Félicité de 19
'Land and Liberty' (Russian secret
  society) 87
Laplace, Pierre de 23
L'Avenir (journal) 19
Ledru-Rollin, Alexandre 111, 112
Le Moniteur 70
Leopold I, king of Belgium 52
Lermontov, Mikhail 25, 81
Le Verrier, Urbain 23
Liberal Catholic movement,
  formation of (1829) 19
Liberty Leading the People (Delacroix)
  109
Liebig, Justus von 23
Light Brigade, Charge of the *67*, 74
Liverpool, Lord 30
Lloyd's (insurance house) *26*
London, conference of (1830) 52;
  conference of (1841) 71; Treaty of
  (1827) 66; Treaty of (1840) 71–2
London Working Men's Association,
  founded (1836) 38
Louis I of Bavaria *44*, 58
Louis XVI, king of France 95
Louis XVIII, king of France 26, 45, 97;
  restored to the throne (1815) 93–4, *95*,
  96
Louis Bonaparte. *see* Napoleon III
Louis Philippe, king of France 12, 17,
  33, 49, 50, 52, 61, 71, 99, 100, 101,
  102, 103, 105, 108, 119
Lucknow 38
Luddite rising 18
L'Univers 123

MacMahon, General 74
Macpherson, James 24
Mahmud, Sultan 70, 71
Mahratta chiefs 39
Malakoff, fortification of 73; battle
  for 74
Malthus, Reverend Thomas 34
Mameluke mercenaries 69
Manin, Daniele 54, 58
Maoris 41
Marmont, General 98–9
Martignac, Viscount 99
Marx, Karl 17, *19*, 22, 42, 61, 82, 86,
  106, 111, 123
Mary Stuart (Schiller) 22
Maupas, C. E. de 115
Mavrokordatos, Alexander 66, 67
Maximilian, king of Bavaria 58
Mazzini, Giuseppe 49–50, 58, 59, 112
Mehemet Ali, Pasha of Egypt 64, 66, 67,
  68–9, 71, 72
Melbourne, Lord 35
Memoirs (Saint-Simon) 21
Menshikov, Prince 73
Mesta 10
Metternich, Prince 42, 45, 48, 50, *53*, 57,
  62, 66
Miaoules, Andreas *63*, 66
Mill, John Stuart 12
Mir (Russian village council) 84
Missolonghi, battle of (1826) 68
Modena, Duke of 54
Monge, Gaspard 22

Montalembert, Count of 19
Mont Cenis tunnel 121
Montez, Lola *44*
Montijo, Eugénie of 117, *118*
Morny, Duke of 115, *120*
Morse, Samuel 23
Municipal Corporations Act (1835) 35
Municipal Guard (French) *109*

Naples, revolution in (1820) 45-8
Napoleon I 24, 25, *49*, 70, 75, 76, 95, 98,
  99, 104, *109*
Napoleon III 73, 74, 104, 115, 117, 119,
  120, 124; accession 54; *coup d'état*
  (1851) *114*, 115-17, 120; marriage 117,
  118; reforms 122
National Assembly, in France 111, 115,
  122, 124
National Assembly, in Germany *55, 59*
National Guard (French) 98, 100, 103,
  105, 106
National Workshops 108-9, 111, 120
Navarino, battle of (1827) *64*, 66, 70
Navigation Acts, repeal of (1848) 41
Nemours, Duke of 52
New Harmony (social community in
  U.S.A.) 21
New Lanark Mills, reforms at 36
New Moral View of Society (Owen) 21
Newton, Isaac 23
Ney, Marshal 94
Nezib, battle of 71
Nicholas I, Tsar 59, 62, 73, 76-7, *78*, 79,
  80, 82, *84*, 88
Niepce, Nicéphore *19*
Nightmare (Fuseli) 24
Novara, battle of (1849) *51*, 58
Novgorod, revolt in 79

Obrenovich, Miloš 64
O'Connell, Daniel *29*, 32, 33
O'Connor, Feargus 38
Oersted, Hans Christian 23
Ollivier, Emile 124
Olmutz, Treaty of 62
Opium War (1840-2) 40
Orange Free State 41
Order of Maria Theresa *16*
Order of the Garter *30*
Orléanists, victory of 99-100
Orléans, Duke of 98
Orsini Affair 121-2
Ossian 24
Otto I, king of Greece 69
Ottoman Empire. *see* Turkey
Owen, Robert 21, 36, 42
Ozanam, Frederick 19

Palacký, František *55*, 57, 58
Palikares 64
Palmerston, Lord 71, 72, 74
Pan-Slav congress *55*
Paris, rebuilding of 120-1
Paris, Treaty of (1856) 74, 82, 121
Parliamentary reform in England 33
Parma, duke of 54
Pasha Rashid, Grand Vizier 70
Paul I, Tsar 75
Peel, Robert 15, 17, 27, 32, 38, 39
People's Charter, The (1837) 38
Pepe, General 48
Périer, Casimir 15, 100, 103
Pestel, Colonel 76, 77, *81*
Peterloo Massacre (1819) 30
Peter the Great 75
Petrachevists 81
Philosophical Radicals 33
Pitt, William 25
Pius IX, Pope 54, 57, 58-9
Polacky, Frantisek *55*, 57, 58
Poland, guerrilla warfare (1863) 88;
  insurrection 88, 89; liberalism 50;
  rising (1830) 79
Polignac, Auguste de 97-8
Poor Law Amendment Act (1834) 34-5,
  38
Prague *55*, 58, 59
Proudhon, Pierre Joseph 21, 106
Punch 38
Pushkin, Alexander 81, *83*, 90

Radetzky, Marshal *51*, 58-9
Radicalism 27, 30
Raspail, François 100
Récamier, Madame *48*
Reform Bill (1832) 17, 33-4, 35

Republicans in France 100, 103, 105,
  106, 108, 112, 123, 124
Revolution of 1830 49, 50
Revolutions of 1848 54-62
Rhine Gazette 61
Ricardo, David 12
Richelieu, Duc de 95
Riego, Colonel 45, 49
Rochefort, Henri 124
Rossi, Count 58
Rothschild 15, 17
Rue de Rohan, battle of 101
Russia, abolition of serfdom 82-4;
  defeat in Crimean War 75; economic
  development in 90; expansion of
  empire 89; influence on Balkans 70-1;
  industrial revolution in 79-80;
  intelligentsia in 81-2; invaded by
  France (1821) 75; reforms 82-6;
  repression 78; revolutionary activity
  76-7, 86-8; secret societies 87;
  standard of living 90-1; war with
  Turkey 73-4
Russia and the Russians (Turgenev) 81
Russian Orthodox Church 74, 88
Ryleiev, Kondrati 76

Sadowa, battle of 123
Saint-Arnaud, Armand de 115
Saint-Hilaire, Auguste de 24
Saint-Simon, Count of 16, 19, 21, 106
Saint Vincent de Paul (religious society)
  19, 123
Sand, Karl Ludwig *44*
Sauerbronn, Baron von *13*
Say, Jean Baptiste 12
Schiller, Friedrich von *22*, 24
Schwarzenberg, Prince Felix 62
Scientific Revolution 22
Scott, Sir Walter 24
'Seasons, The' (secret society in
  France) 103
Sebastopol, battle of 73-4
Second Empire *120*, 121
Sedan, battle of 93
Senior, Nassau 34
Serbia, independence of 69
Serbs, revolution of (1815) 64
Serfdom, abolition in Russia (1861) *86*,
  82, 84, *87*, 90, 92
Shaftesbury, Lord 36
Shelley, Percy Bysshe 24
Slavery, abolished in British Empire 35;
  abolished in South Africa (1833) 36
Slitzweg, Karl *22*
Smith, Adam 12
Sobraon, battle of (1846) *38*
Socialism, in England 20, 21, 22; in
  France 106, 108, 109, 112, 124
Society for the Rights of Man 103, *104*
Soult, General 103
Souvenirs from the House of the Dead
  (Dostoevsky) 82
Spain 48
Speenhamland System 30
Speranksi, Count Mikhail 75, 78
Statute of Westminster (1931) 41
Steinheil, Carl von 23
Stephens, Joseph 38
Stephenson, George 15
Stratford de Redcliffe, Lord 73
Suez Canal 121
Suvorov, Count Alexander 78
Syrian War, First 70-1; Second 71-2

Talleyrand 95, 98
Tanzimat 71, 72
Tashkent, capture of 89
Telegraph system, construction of 16, 23
Test Acts, repealed (1828) 32
The Idiot (Dostoevsky) 81
The Possessed (Dostoevsky) 87
The Prisoner of the Caucasus (Pushkin)
  81
Thiers, Adolphe 98, 103, 115, 123
'Third Party, The' 124
Tischbein, Johann Heinrich Wilhelm *20*
Tolpuddle Martyrs (1834) 36
Tommaseo, Niccolo 54
Trade Unions 18, 30, 36-7
Transport, revolution in 15-16
Transvaal, Republic of 40
Troppau, congress of (1820) 48-9
Troubetzkoy, Prince Paul 76
Turgenev, Ivan 81
Turkey 62-4; British influence 71;
  decline 72; French influence 72; naval

blockade of 66; reforms in 72; war
  with Egypt 70-1; war with Greece
  64-9; war with Russia 73

Ultra-Royalist party (in France) 95, 97
Unkiar-Skelessi, secret treaty of 70, 72
Uvarov, Count 78

Verona, Congress of (1822) 49
Victor Emmanuel I, king of Sardinia 48,
  59
Victoria, queen of England *30, 33*, 35,
  41
Victoria of Leiningen, Princess 35
Vienna, congress of 45, *46*
Vienna, revolution in (1848) 53, 56
Villèle, Count of 94, 96-8
Volonskaya, Maria *81*
Volosts 84
Volta, Alessandro 23

Wallachia, rising in 67
Wallis, George Auguste 20
Waterloo, battle of 10, *24*, 25, 95
Watt, James 11
Wealth of Nations (Smith) 12
Weitling (German revolutionary) 22
Wellington, Arthur Wellesley, Duke of
  24, 30, 32, 38, 70
Whigs 26, 33, 34, 39
Wilberforce, William 35
William IV, king of England *29*, 34, 35
William of Orange 52, 99
Windischgraetz, Marshal 59
Winterhalter, Franz *30*
Witte, Count 92

Young Ireland party 33
'Young Russia' (Russian secret society)
  87
Ypsilanti, Alexander 65

Zemstovs (Russian councils) 84, 86, 92
Zollverein (customs union) 50, 61;
  development of 15-16